NATURAL BORN FEEDER

WHOLE FOODS, WHOLE LIFE

NATURAL

BORN

FEEDER

Whole Foods, Whole Life

ROZ PURCELL

GILL BOOKS

Gill Books
Hume Avenue
Park West
Dublin 12
www.gillbooks.ie

Gill Books is an imprint of M.H. Gill & Co.

© Rozanna Purcell 2016

978 07171 6817 0

In collaboration with Kristin Jensen
Designed by www.grahamthew.com
Photography © Joanne Murphy
Food and props styled by Jette Virdi
Indexed by Eileen O'Neill
Printed by BZ Graf. S.A. Poland

PROPS
Industry: 41a/b Drury Street, Dublin 2; T: (01) 613 9111;
E: hello@industryandco.com; www.industrydesign.ie
Article: Powerscourt Townhouse, South William Street, Dublin
2; T: (01) 679 9268; E: items@articledublin.com;
www.articledublin.com
Two Wooden Horses: www.twowoodenhorses.com

This book is typeset in 9 on 13pt Fedra Serif.

The paper used in this book comes from the wood pulp of
managed forests. For every tree felled, at least one tree is
planted, thereby renewing natural resources.

A CIP catalogue record for this book is available from the
British Library.

5 4 3 2

THE AUTHOR

Roz Purcell began blogging at naturalbornfeeder.com in 2013 to
document her love of cooking and to share her recipes. No stranger
to television audiences, she won *Celebrity Come Dine with Me* (Ireland) in
2012 and regularly appears on TV3's *Xposé*. Roz is also one of Ireland's
most successful models and the 2010 winner of Miss Universe Ireland.
Originally from Co. Tipperary, she now lives in Dublin.

ACKNOWLEDGEMENTS

I would like to start by thanking Gill Books for giving me the opportunity to create this book and share my food journey with you. I am extremely grateful to have had this opportunity. A special thanks to my commissioning editor, Deirdre Nolan, who supported me throughout this process and was very hands on in all elements of crafting the book. Also thanks to Catherine Gough, Sarah Liddy and Teresa Daly for all of your help and support.

To my perfect 'shoot team', Joanne Murphy and Jette Virdi, you truly helped to create my dream book. Working alongside you helped develop my own personal food style and I learned so much. Your precision and hard work was very inspiring. Thanks also to Graham Thew for a wonderful book design.

To my editor, Kristin Jensen, the ultimate teammate. Kristin never failed to encourage and help promote my own writing style by carefully editing every last word. Your guidance through this process is something that made my first book experience wonderful, but also valuable for my future writing endeavors.

Most of all I would like to thank my grandmother, who has been and will always be such an inspiration to me. Without her wonderful passion for food, her 'feeding' nature and her fun approach to creating memories in the kitchen, I would have never developed such a strong love for cooking and baking.

To my parents and aunties for always involving me in the cooking process and instilling a wholefood philosophy in my life. For putting up with years of messy kitchens and cleaning up afterwards (never my strong point!).

Two of my favourite food bloggers, Imen McDonnell and Caitriona Redmond, who encouraged me to share my passion and helped me to take the first step to start Natural Born Feeder, your enthusiasm was and still is contagious!

To anyone who has ever followed the blog or simply recreated one of my recipes. It is something that never fails to excite me and it reinforces why I am doing what I do. The interest and support is something that I have never experienced before. It is heartwarming and, most of all, motivates me to keep experimenting and creating new recipes to share with you.

CONTENTS

MAIN DISHES

TURKEY AND CHICKEN

LAMB AND BEEF

SEAFOOD

VEGETARIAN

FAKE-AWAY

SIMPLE PLEASURES

SWEET SNACKS

SPORTS SNACKS

DIPS AND THINGS

THE NUT BUTTER COLLECTIVE

INTRODUCTION

I've had a roller coaster relationship with food. From growing up on a farm to living on coffee when I was modelling in New York to developing my whole foods philosophy, I've been through the whole spectrum.

Working in an industry for the past seven years that is based solely on aesthetics derailed my passion for food. Food became the enemy and was something to be avoided as much as possible. I didn't know anything about nutrition or healthy eating, so I fell into one cliché after another. You don't have to be a model to go through all that, though. In this age of social media, we all feel the pressure to be picture perfect all of the time.

But now, at the age of 24, I consider myself to be very fortunate to have found my passion. Food is my way of creating, sharing and unwinding and of being more in the present. Cooking and baking have helped me to realise that life is about the simple pleasures of everyday moments.

EARLY DAYS

Growing up, I had a great outlook when it came to food. My parents made a conscious effort to keep processed foods out of the house, and along with my grandmother, they taught me how to cook. I was making my own school lunches and dinners from the age of six. My mother was the school principal and had a strict healthy eating policy, though I sometimes snuck some chocolate into my lunchbox – I was the last person she would suspect!

Food was part of our family traditions and was something to be celebrated.

Sunday dinners were always a big deal. My grandfather's hobby was fishing, so fresh fish was always a feature, mashed potatoes were unlimited and a side table would be groaning under the weight of all the desserts. There are hardly any photos of me in my youth without a piece of cake in my hand or mouth. Saying that, though, I was a very active child. I played on every local team, from camogie to tennis, and rarely sat still long enough to watch TV.

The area I grew up in at the foot of Slievenamon in Tipperary was also a haven of good-quality local produce. Some of my fondest memories are of calling to my neighbours to collect eggs, learning about beekeeping from another neighbour who supplied us with raw honey and picking our own apples to make apple jelly.

I grew up spending most of my time with my grandmother, Aida, who passed on her passion for baking to me. It was, and still is, my main connection with her. She taught me how to make everything from roux-based sauces to homemade marshmallows and she spoiled my sisters and I with three-course homemade meals, freshly baked breads and every kind of cake a child could imagine.

Learning how to cook and bake turned out to be one of the greatest gifts I've ever been given. As a child, I viewed food as an art. It allowed me to be creative and to make other people happy. Being able to cook for myself and others has made me want to inspire others in turn to make better food choices and rethink food.

I had a wonderful relationship with food and it was a vital part of my family. It was how we would celebrate, create and simply spend time together. But that all changed.

THE VICIOUS CIRCLE

When I started modelling and travelling abroad for work at age 18, I found myself adopting bizarre food fads and eating routines. I felt like I had no choice and no time. I was under huge pressure not to waste this chance and I didn't want to fail. I was young and impressionable, so of course I tried every wondrous new diet and fast fix around. I started to blame food for any of my physical issues and struggles with my measurements. I stopped baking and cooking and caring about food, and I lost my hobby and creative outlet in the process.

Coming from a background where I never deprived myself or put too much thought into what I ate, I had no idea what I was supposed to do or eat now in this new world. I would go through phases of splurging and fasting, or I would wait long periods between eating and skip meals, then punish myself with hard runs when I thought I had stepped out of line – even though I didn't know what the line was or where it was supposed to be.

Despite working in an industry based on looks, no one ever gave me any advice on what or how to eat. When I was just starting out I couldn't afford to get personal training, particularly when I was abroad, and any 'advice' I was given usually came from people who needed to get fast results and didn't really care about the long term. When I would return home from travelling I would inevitably put back on all the weight I had lost, and then some. This vicious circle continued for a few years, until it all came to a head in 2011 when I decided to stop travelling. For the first time in ages, there was no pressure, no deadlines.

There were some plus sides to my travels, though. I've learned a lot from spending time in different cultures and I've picked up so many tips from working and living with models from all over the world. Participating in the Miss Universe competition in 2010 was a big game changer. I saw a new image of what the 'perfect' body was: it had abs and was very toned, which was way more achievable than a frail, thin frame for me. I trained in Colombia for three weeks prior to the competition in Las Vegas, which lasted for four weeks, and I remember going over thinking, *Here we go, be prepared to be hungry*. I was happily surprised when my pageant coaches emphasised the importance of eating frequently. They helped me prepare meals every three hours and introduced me to weight training. I started calling in to health food stores and would spend up to an hour asking about all the different foods I had never seen before, from quinoa (remember, this was in 2010) to umeboshi. I suddenly realised that there was a whole other food world out there – I just hadn't explored it yet.

Unfortunately, by the time I returned to Ireland I had developed an underactive thyroid. Worst of all, I knew it was all self-inflicted from my years of bad choices. All I heard were the words *lethargic* and *weight gain* – the very things I'd spent the past three years trying to avoid.

TIME FOR A CHANGE

I've never been the best at taking medicine, so after three months of half-empty packs of pills left to one side, I knew something had to change, and that it had to be my lifestyle. Learning from my past mistakes of going for an all-or-nothing approach, this time I decided to make slow, small, attainable changes over a long period of time instead.

I started by altering my training and eating patterns. Training had been a big part of my life already. I played any and every sport as a child and teenager and ran every day throughout my early twenties (I have the bad knees now to prove it) before a few running injuries compelled me to take up cycling instead. I adapted my training to two short sessions of 30 minutes a day, five days a week. Plus I started to eat regularly and cook everything from scratch – pretty much all the things everyone always tells you to do but can seem like too much effort.

But my biggest change was a mental one. I started to focus on what I *could* eat rather than on what I couldn't. This changed everything. I realised that by eating whole foods, I wasn't missing much anyway. By changing my lifestyle and diet, I managed to get my thyroid condition under control in a little under a year.

But my up-and-down journey with food wasn't over yet. From not caring about food at all, I swung to the opposite end of the spectrum and became too concerned and conscious about it. I became obsessed with finding the 'perfect' diet. I began cutting things out of my diet, from single foods to entire food groups. I read about different diets all over the world and the latest research on all the foods that supposedly are going to kill you. I wanted to see everything being prepared and insisted on knowing every last detail about the food before I put it in my mouth. Let's just say I wasn't much fun to go out to dinner with.

I had to take a step back and try to be more rational. There were times I knew I wasn't getting enough nutrition out of my diet, but I was overanalysing food so much that

I couldn't enjoy it. I would go for long training rides with friends, but when we would stop for a coffee I would freak out because I couldn't possibly eat anything on the menu. I finally realised that I needed to cop on when I went out for a meal with my dad and got really upset because there was nothing I would eat on the menu in a perfectly good restaurant. I had taken all the enjoyment out of food again by searching for this mythical 'perfect' diet.

Deciding to do a triathlon in 2013 helped me to return to a better baseline. All of a sudden, I had to fuel my body with more than just aesthetics in mind. Going through that training helped me learn what foods are needed, why and when. For example, I learned why carb loading for particularly long training days or events is necessary and how my pre- and post-race meals could benefit my performance. My focus shifted from how food was going to make me look to how it was going to help me perform, recover and progress.

From all this, I eventually learned that there is no one 'perfect' diet. Everyone is different, so it should come as no surprise that food affects us all differently. What works for one person might not have the same results for you. All you can do is experiment and learn what works for *you*. Start by educating yourself and your palate to find what works best, what you like and what satisfies you. A sustainable, healthy lifestyle isn't about extremes. It's all about balance.

WHOLE FOODS FOR A WHOLE LIFE

Like most models, I still have an important relationship with food. The big difference now, though, is that I don't buy into any restrictive do's or dont's. Instead, I like to follow a few simple, sustainable guidelines.

When it comes to food, I take an 80/20 approach. This helps me to have a manageable balance and a sustainable lifestyle, but it also filters out the guilt. When you're enjoying that 20%, go ahead and really enjoy it! Allow yourself that treat and know that 80% of the time you're nourishing your body with healthy, wholesome foods. I still find it hard to let go of that guilt, though; I think a lot of health-conscious people do. It can be hard to move on from that meal and get over it, but remember, no one is perfect all the time.

I make an extra effort to source my foods well and I try to buy foods that are in season. We have some of the world's best food producers here in Ireland, so take advantage of it and look for quality. Sourcing is an important part of a whole, balanced approach. For example, you don't have to cut out animal products if you like them – just try to be mindful of where you source them from.

I also avoid processed food for the simple reasons that I can't pronounce half the ingredients, it alters my mood and because I've become a lot more conscious about what I'm putting into my body rather than what's showing on the outside.

But if you take away only one message from this book, I hope it's this: *cook from scratch*. Cooking from scratch is the most important aspect of my food philosophy. When you cook from scratch, you see and touch every ingredient that's going into the end result. Cooking from scratch gives you greater choice, and it's a lot easier to make that choice than standing in the supermarket aisles trying to decipher the long lists of unpronounceable ingredients on labels.

I know this can be easier said than done, but I believe that everyone can at least make a few basics. Try starting with something simple, like hummus one week or your own homemade granola bars the next. Pick one recipe a week and master it, then play around with it to make it your own. There's something for everyone in this book, no matter what your budget is or how busy you are.

NATURAL BORN FEEDER IS BORN

When I set up my blog, Natural Born Feeder, back in 2013, I didn't have an agenda. I just started it as a way to document my MacGyver moments in the kitchen and to keep a record of my recipes. Because something else had started to happen during this time – I started making my own recreations of the things I did miss. I'm not going to lie; I crave a Mars bar or a pizza as much as the next person. But now I make the treats I miss with whole foods, and you know what? I don't even miss the original versions anymore.

I get such a buzz out of people recreating my recipes, and sometimes my blog readers even challenge me to recreate their favourite cheat meal, takeaway or dessert. I love making old favourites in a way that hasn't been done before, with new ingredients. I love seeing my readers start their shift towards leading a healthier lifestyle and I'm happy to be a part of it.

Sometimes I'd post pictures of edible gifts or hampers that I had made for friends, things like my protein balls or bar, and people would email me asking where they could buy them. I never really entertained the idea of doing a line of products because more than anything, I want to encourage people to do it themselves and realise just how easy it is to create simple, tasty, healthy food. Plus I was still shocked that people actually liked my blog, never mind the fact that they were interested in buying products. And yet, when I would have long working days in town or would meet friends for a meal, I'd always worry about where I'd be able to get healthy food that I could trust and believe in.

It just so happened that I was asked to launch the opening of Mooch, a frozen yoghurt shop on Dawson Street. I met the owners and we instantly bonded over our love of good food, and we started collaborating in 2014. We started with some breakfast options and the menu has grown to include a range of smoothies, raw protein balls, overnight oats on the go and granola bars along with the oat pancakes and vegan waffles we kicked off with. These days you'll often find me in the Mooch kitchen creating new recipes or even making some of my NBF pancakes.

Because of my blog, I've made so many new friends and have met and worked with people who all share the same passion to encourage people to make better food choices. Even though I write the blog on my own, I feel like I have a fantastic network and support team behind me. Nothing makes me happier than meeting someone who follows my blog and gives me their feedback. At one of my cooking demos a woman came up to me and said, 'My kitchen is a mess because of you! My 16-year-old daughter follows your blog and now she has started her very own.' It made my day. It's incredible to think that the things I love doing – cooking and baking and blogging – are encouraging other people to learn about food and get creative with it, who then inspire others in turn.

Writing my blog made me realise just how much I cook and bake and what a big part of my life it is, and the *Natural Born Feeder* book has only reinforced that. Writing this book has made me clearly outline my food values and why I stand strong over them and my approach to food. After all

those tumultuous years of going from one extreme to the next, I'm finally happy and satisfied with where I'm at with food. Writing this cookbook has made me realise that I'm in the right place and that I'm ready to move on to the next chapter.

WHAT'S NEXT

It's a little overwhelming to think that people are actually listening to what I say, and it makes me feel that I have somewhat of a duty to my readers. Natural Born Feeder is a space where people can get recipes but also educate themselves a bit more about what it takes to create a sustainable, healthy lifestyle. I want to use that platform as well as I can and share as much as possible, which is one of the reasons why I'm going back to college to study nutrition. There's still so much more that I want to learn about food and I can't wait to share it with my readers. I'm constantly thinking about what's next in my food journey and I firmly believe that with enough hard work, what's right for me will happen.

I never would have guessed that I'd end up where I have when it comes to food. After all the ups and downs I've gone through, I have finally achieved a healthy, sustainable lifestyle and a healthy relationship with food. It just goes to show that no matter how much you might fight it, your true passion will always prevail and the rest will follow.

SYMBOLS USED IN THIS BOOK

Most of the recipes in this book are dairy free, gluten free, paleo and/or vegan.

D dairy free   P paleo

G gluten free   V vegan

A NATURAL BORN FEEDER PANTRY

My weekly shop changes depending on the season. I also try to buy Irish produce as much as possible, not only for the taste and freshness but also for its traceability. My pantry and fridge are usually stocked with the following foods.

FRUIT

apples
avocados
bananas
berries
dried apricots
goji berries
lemons
limes
Medjool dates
raw mulberries

VEG

broccoli
carrots
cauliflower
celery
courgettes
cucumbers
garlic
green beans
onions
peppers
spinach
sweet potatoes
tomatoes

GRAINS

brown rice
buckwheat groats
bulgur wheat
quinoa
steel-cut oats

NUTS AND SEEDS

almonds
cashews
flaxseeds
hazelnuts
hemp seeds
macadamia nuts
pecans
pistachios
psyllium husk
pumpkin seeds
sesame seeds
sunflower seeds
walnuts

MEAT, POULTRY AND EGGS

organic chicken
 (different cuts)
organic, free-range
 eggs
turkey breast, fillet
 or minced

FISH

hake
mackerel
prawns
salmon

DAIRY

feta cheese
grass-fed butter
natural yoghurt

BEANS AND LEGUMES

black beans
chickpeas
lentils

SWEETENERS

coconut nectar
maple syrup
raw honey
powdered stevia

FRESH HERBS

basil
coriander
dill
mint
parsley
rosemary
thyme

SPICES

cardamom
cayenne
chilli
cinnamon
cloves
coriander
cumin
ginger
mustard seeds
nutmeg
paprika
sumac
turmeric

OILS

coconut oil
flaxseed oil
rapeseed oil
sesame oil

OTHER

apple cider vinegar
balsamic apple cider
 vinegar
brown rice protein
 powder
cacao nibs
mirin
miso
nori wraps
nutritional yeast
olives
raw cacao powder
tahini
tamari
umeboshi plums
whey protein
 powder

WHERE TO SHOP

Investing a little time at the start to research the best places to shop in your area will be time well spent. Whatever your priorities are – whether it's superfood vs. local food – there are ways to work within whatever your budget is.

SUPERMARKETS

In the past few years, most of the big supermarket chains in Ireland have made an effort to support Irish produce and small producers. And now that they are recognising the growing interest in health foods, they are also giving shelf space to items that previously could only be found in specialty or health food stores.

FARMERS' MARKETS

There are farmers' markets all over the country, so find your nearest one and take some time out of your weekend to stop by. People tend to think that farmers' markets are expensive, but that's not the case. I get great-quality eggs, fish and veg at a much lower cost than at the supermarket. Plus it's always nice to meet the people behind the product! Farmers' markets are a great way to support your local producers, whether they make honey, cheese, yoghurt, cider vinegars or grow fruit and veg. Shop local to make sure these top-quality producers – and their food – stick around.

ASIAN MARKETS

You might not think it, but Asian markets are brilliant places to buy spices, nuts and grains in bulk at a good price. They can be hard to navigate sometimes, but once you get to know the store, you'll be glad you did.

FISHMONGER

Fish is an important part of my diet, so I want to make sure I'm getting the best. I go to a fishmonger for spanking fresh fish at better prices than you'd get pre-packed fish for at a supermarket. Plus you can put your fishmonger's expertise to work for you – ask them to skin and debone fish fillets or peel and devein prawns for you.

GROW YOUR OWN

Anyone can grow a few herbs, even if, like me, your 'garden' is just a windowsill in a city flat.

ESSENTIAL KITCHEN KIT

These are the appliances, big and small, that I'd be lost without.

FOOD PROCESSOR

A good-quality, powerful food processor is an excellent investment that will make all your kitchen tasks that much easier. It not only saves time and work, but it also allows you to make things like flours, nut butters, nut milks or even ice creams. I use a Thermomix. Yes, it has a hefty price tag, but I use it every day so I've definitely got good value from it.

JUICER

I'm not a big juicer, but a good juice can really complement a meal and it's a fantastic way to get tons of nutrients packed into one glass. Plus a juicer can also make tasty cordials and fresh power shots (I particularly love a beetroot shot during my training season). I use a masticating juicer for a number of reasons. Firstly, it's the only juicer that can juice wheatgrass and some other leafy greens. It also yields a more nutrient-rich raw juice by twisting the fruit and vegetables, which breaks down the fibres very slowly – but don't worry, it doesn't take ages to make the juice. But most importantly – and this is my favourite part – it's actually really easy to clean.

JULIENNE PEELER

A julienne peeler is a cheaper option than a spiraliser and is a good alternative if you don't have much storage space in your kitchen. I used one before buying my spiraliser, and I still use it. It gives similar results but is hand held, small and easy to use.

NUTRIBULLET

A powerful little machine packed into a unique, slim design that's very easy to clean to boot. It can even blend whole root veg. In addition to the usual smoothies, I also use it for making some of my pancake batters, date caramel and nut milks and for making flours too, like oat and quinoa flour. Considering how much I use it, it's been my number one best-value kitchen purchase.

MANDOLINE SLICER

If you eat a lot of veggies and raw foods, a mandolin is a great way to cut vegetables thinly and precisely. Just watch your fingers because those blades are super sharp – something I've learned the hard way.

NON-STICK PAN

A must for pancakes, crêpes, egg wraps and much more. Depending on the brand, the quality and how well you take care of your pan, you might need to buy a new one every year. If you own a good non-stick pan, make sure you're treating it right.

PESTLE AND MORTAR

A good, heavy-duty pestle and mortar is a handy tool for grinding spices and seeds and for crushing nuts – and, of course, for making guacamole. Spice is an important element of healthy eating, as it boosts flavour as well as nutritional content.

SLOW COOKER

Slow cookers are such a helpful way of cooking and are inexpensive and easy to find too. Just prepare the veg and meat in the morning, throw it into the slow cooker and forget about it until it's time for dinner. They're a lifesaver for busy people who want to arrive home at the end of a long day to a wholesome dinner.

SPIRALISER

A nifty kitchen gadget that makes veggies into noodles – what more do I need to say? It's a good tool to trick the mind and senses and it makes food fun.

THE LITTLE HELPERS

AIRTIGHT CONTAINERS: Essential for storing your leftovers and baked goods, but make sure you only put food in a container once it is completely cool. Otherwise the steam that the food keeps giving off will condense in the container and make it soggy.

BAKING TINS: From standard cake tins to loaf tins and specialty tins for bagels or donuts, a good tin will last for ages, so start your collection now.

CHOPPING BOARDS: Take a tip from the pros and get a complete chopping board set, with a different board for each food group – handy and hygienic.

COFFEE GRINDER: A coffee grinder also works perfectly for milling nuts and seeds.

GARLIC PRESS OR GRINDER: In short, it makes garlic fun.

GLASS JARS: Keep all your old jam jars and reuse them for storage, overnight oats, nut butters and for stashing trail mix in.

HAND-HELD BLENDER: A compact, useful tool for soups, sauces and smoothies.

KITCHEN SCALES: No 'guestimation' allowed here! Scales are particularly important when baking, which requires more accuracy.

KNIVES: Put a good knife – or even a whole set – on your Christmas list. A good knife saves time and maybe even your fingers too. Make sure you keep your knives sharp, as you're more likely to cut yourself with a dull knife than a sharp one because a dull knife has a greater chance of slipping.

MUSLIN CLOTH: Cheap and multipurpose, these are commonly used when making nut milks.

PIZZA CUTTER: Great for neatly shaping dough, crackers and, of course, cutting pizza.

SMALL STEPS

TO SUCCESS

1
-
Keep your kitchen stocked with healthy snack options so that you never go hungry.

2
-
Know your weaknesses – and maybe try to make a healthier version.

3
-
Forgive yourself if you slip up. Just say to yourself 'I really enjoyed that', then move on and put it behind you.

4
-
Cut out processed food (refined carbs, sugars, trans fats) slowly but surely.

5
-
Add a little more veg and fibre to your diet.

6
-
Encourage others you live or work with to start making healthy choices too.

7
-
Take up a sport, join a team or start a class to be a part of something and to stay motivated.

8
-
Educate yourself on what you're eating.

9
-
Pick at least one recipe a week to make from scratch and share.

10
-
And remember: keep food fun!

SMOOTHIES, JUICES, NON-DAIRY MILKS AND DRINKS

These recipes will keep you – and your fridge!
– full. Once you realise how easy it is to make
your own smoothies, juices and milks, you'll never
drink shop-bought ones again.

SMOOTHIES

HONEY I'M HOME SMOOTHIE

This is my favourite smoothie by far. It's so creamy and sweet, it's almost like a dessert and it's perfect for any season. Drink it immediately for the best taste. **SERVES 1**

100g baby spinach

½ ripe avocado, peeled and stoned

125ml fresh apple juice

juice of ½ lemon

2.5cm piece of fresh root ginger (unpeeled if using a high-speed blender)

1 tbsp honey

bee pollen, to garnish

Put all the ingredients into a powerful blender and blitz until smooth. Pour into a glass and sprinkle with bee pollen to garnish.

GET UP AND GOJI SMOOTHIE

A little something to wake you up and help you 'beet' the Monday blues! The beetroot in this smoothie can be cooked or raw, depending on how powerful your blender is.

SERVES 1

1 small beetroot, cooked or raw (see note above)

2 tbsp goji berries

125g fresh or frozen raspberries

100g fresh or frozen strawberries, hulled if fresh

1 Medjool date, pitted

2.5cm piece of fresh root ginger

250ml fresh apple juice

3 fresh mint leaves or lemon balm leaves, to garnish

If you're using raw beetroot, peel it and cut it into quarters. Place the goji berries in a bowl, cover them with water and soak for 10 minutes to soften them. Drain and place in a powerful blender with all the other ingredients and blitz until smooth. Pour into a glass and garnish with the fresh mint or lemon balm leaves.

G V P D

STRAWBERRIES AND CREAM SMOOTHIE

The perfect smoothie for all you milkshake lovers out there. Get a head start on this the night before by freezing the banana slices, which will make your smoothie extra creamy.

SERVES 1

1 banana, peeled, cut into discs and frozen

250g fresh strawberries, hulled

250ml unsweetened almond milk

1 tbsp cashew butter

Place all the ingredients into a powerful blender and blitz until smooth.

PURE PASSION SMOOTHIE

This is so fresh and light and tropical, you'll want to add it to your regular summer repertoire. For a really refreshing drink, freeze the banana ahead of time. **SERVES 2**

1 banana, peeled

1 passion fruit, pulp only, with some seeds reserved as garnish

250ml freshly squeezed orange juice

250ml fresh pineapple juice

Place all the ingredients into a powerful blender and blitz until smooth. Pour into a glass and garnish with passion fruit seeds.

EASY PLEASER SMOOTHIE

SERVES 1

1 banana, peeled
....

6 red grapes
....

250ml coconut milk
....

1 tsp raw cacao powder
....

Place all the ingredients into a powerful blender and blitz until smooth.

CHOCOLATE CHIP SHAKE

I made this for my sister one day during Lent to help her combat her chocolate cravings. It did the job, but now I have to make it for her all the time! **SERVES 1**

2 Medjool dates, pitted

½ ripe avocado, peeled and stoned

250ml unsweetened almond milk

2 tbsp cacao nibs, plus extra to garnish

1 tbsp raw cacao powder

1 tbsp coconut oil

1 tsp maca powder

pinch of desiccated coconut, to garnish

fresh mint leaf, to garnish

Place all the ingredients except the desiccated coconut and mint leaf into a powerful blender and blitz until smooth. Pour into a glass and garnish with a sprinkle of desiccated coconut and a fresh mint leaf.

 G V P D

PROTEIN-PACKED SMOOTHIES

BIG FACE SMOOTHIE

I named this after my boyfriend. It's the perfect smoothie for someone who needs to chill out! **SERVES 1**

100g baby spinach

½ ripe avocado, peeled and stoned

8 fresh mint leaves

2.5cm piece of fresh root ginger

1 scoop (30g) vanilla whey protein powder

250ml coconut water

juice of ½ lime

handful of ice cubes

Place all the ingredients into a powerful blender and blitz until smooth. If your blender isn't that strong, leave out the ice and add it to the glass instead.

NATURAL BORN FUELLER

This is my post-workout smoothie, but it's also a favourite among my friends and Mooch fans. **SERVES 1**

1 banana, peeled
....
3 Medjool dates, pitted
....
1 scoop (30g) vanilla whey protein powder
....
250ml unsweetened almond milk
....
1 tbsp peanut or almond butter
....
1 tsp raw cacao powder (optional)
....
handful of ice cubes
....

Place all the ingredients into a powerful blender and blitz until smooth. If your blender isn't that strong, leave out the ice and add it to the glass instead.

(G)

THE INCREDIBLE HULK SMOOTHIE

SERVES 1

1 pear, unpeeled and cored
....

1 kiwi, peeled
....

1 scoop (30g) hemp protein powder
....

1 vanilla pod, split in half lengthways, seeds scraped out and pod discarded
....

250ml coconut or rice milk
....

1 tbsp honey or maple syrup
....

1 tbsp aloe extract
....

1 tsp freshly squeezed lemon juice
....

Place all the ingredients into a powerful blender and blitz until smooth.

VEGAN if you use maple syrup

BIONIC BURST SMOOTHIE

This smoothie does what it says on the tin. For a major boost pre- or post-gym, this will have you pumped! **SERVES 1**

125g fresh or frozen
blueberries
. . . .

8 fresh or frozen
raspberries
. . . .

8 fresh or frozen
strawberries, hulled if fresh
. . . .

1 banana, peeled
. . . .

1 scoop (30g) hemp protein
powder
. . . .

250ml coconut water
. . . .

1 tbsp coconut oil
. . . .

1 tsp honey or maple syrup
(optional)
. . . .

Place all the ingredients into a powerful blender and blitz until smooth.

VEGAN if you use maple syrup

MATCHA LATTE SMOOTHIE

I started drinking matcha green tea about five years ago and I find that it really helps my mood and energy levels. Try it yourself and see what you think. **SERVES 2**

500ml unsweetened almond milk

1 scoop (30g) whey protein powder

1 tsp matcha green tea

Heat the almond milk in a saucepan until it's a little hotter than you'd like it, as it will cool down in the blender. Add to a blender with the whey protein powder and the matcha tea and blitz until smooth and frothy.

CREAMY ICED MOCHA SMOOTHIE

What a way to start your day! **SERVES 1**

25g raw cacao brown rice protein powder or chocolate whey protein powder

1 banana, peeled, cut into discs and frozen

1 Medjool date, pitted

250ml cashew milk or unsweetened almond milk

1 shot of cold espresso

4 ice cubes

Place all the ingredients into a powerful blender and blitz until smooth and creamy.

JUICES

ORIENT EXPRESS JUICE

SERVES 1

250g fresh pineapple
chunks
....

1 apple, cut into quarters
....

1 lime, peeled and
quartered
....

½ courgette
....

1 stalk of lemongrass
....

Press all the ingredients through a juicer and enjoy.

RUBY RUSH JUICE

MAKES 200ML

1 ruby red grapefruit, peeled
....

1 apple, cut into quarters
....

½ lime, peeled
....

125ml water
....

a few fresh mint leaves, to
serve
....

handful of ice cubes
....

Juice the grapefruit, apple and lime and pour into a glass. Stir in the water and mint leaves and add a handful of ice cubes to serve.

BUBBLY PEAR JUICE

MAKES 600ML

2 pears, cut in half

500ml sparkling water

1 tbsp honey or maple syrup (optional)

crushed ice, to serve

Push the pears through the juicer. Pour the juice into a pitcher and mix in the sparkling water and honey, if using. Serve in glasses over crushed ice.

VEGAN if you use maple syrup

THE MORNING AFTER JUICE

You can guess by its name that this juice will bring you back to life when you need something green to feel normal again. This was my cure after I celebrated my 22nd birthday in a little too much style! **SERVES 1**

50g baby spinach

1 apple, cut into quarters

1 cucumber, cut in half lengthways

2.5cm piece of fresh root ginger

handful of fresh flat-leaf parsley

zest of 1 lemon

250ml coconut water

Press the spinach, apple, cucumber, ginger, parsley and lemon zest through a juicer, then mix with the coconut water.

ADRENALINE JUNKIE JUICE

Turmeric is naturally anti-inflammatory and it also adds a gentle kick to this powerful punch! **MAKES 750ML**

1 lemon, peeled
....

2.5cm piece of fresh root ginger
....

750ml filtered water or coconut water
....

4 fresh mint leaves or lemon balm leaves
....

1 tbsp honey
....

½ tsp ground turmeric
....

pinch of cayenne pepper
....

pinch of sea salt
....

G **P** **D**

Press the lemon and ginger through a juicer. Pour the juice into a pitcher and stir in the filtered water, fresh mint leaves, honey, turmeric, a pinch of cayenne pepper and a pinch of sea salt. Taste and add a little more honey if needed.

DRINKS

WATERMELON SLUSHY

Growing up, I would always get a slushy when I was left to my own devices. They're slightly worrying now when you look at all those day-glo colours, but I think my younger self would approve of this healthier version. **SERVES 1**

550g watermelon chunks, frozen

125ml apple juice or coconut water

handful of fresh mint leaves

1–2 tbsp honey or maple syrup

squeeze of fresh lemon juice

VEGAN if you use maple syrup

Put the frozen watermelon chunks into a powerful blender along with the apple juice, fresh mint, 1 tablespoon of honey and the lemon juice and blend until smooth. Taste and add another tablespoon of honey if you'd like it to be sweeter. Serve immediately and try not to get brain freeze!

RASPBERRY LEMONADE

MAKES 800ML

16 raspberries (set aside 4 to garnish)

4 lemons, zest and pips removed

750ml sparkling water

3 tbsp honey or stevia

VEGAN if you use stevia

Push the raspberries and lemons through a juicer and pour the juice into a pitcher. Mix with the sparkling water and honey and add the remaining whole raspberries.

HOT CHOCOLATE

I'm a bit of a hot chocolate connoisseur, so believe me when I tell you that I've worked long and hard to find the perfect recipe, and this is it. **MAKES 500ML**

500ml oat milk (page 023) or unsweetened almond milk
....

2 tbsp cashew butter
....

2 tbsp maple syrup
....

1 tbsp raw cacao powder
....

1 tsp vanilla essence
....

GLUTEN FREE if you use almond milk

Put the milk into a blender with the cashew butter, maple syrup, cacao powder and vanilla and blitz for 1 minute. Pour into a small saucepan and gently heat for 2 minutes or until it's as warm as you like it. Alternatively, you could zap it in the microwave on high for 2 minutes.

NON-DAIRY MILKS

OAT MILK

MAKES 750ML

90g steel-cut oats

750ml filtered water

½ vanilla pod, split in half lengthways, seeds scraped out and pod discarded, or 1 tsp vanilla essence

2 tbsp maple syrup

Put the oats in a small bowl, cover them with water and let them soak for at least 20 minutes. Drain the oats and rinse them well. Don't be tempted to skip this step or the milk will be slimy!

Place the drained oats in a powerful blender with the filtered water, vanilla seeds and maple syrup and blend on high speed for 1 minute, until the mix is white and smooth.

Line a large bowl with a clean muslin cloth or cheesecloth and pour the oat milk into the cloth. Gather up the cloth, twist the top and use your hands to squeeze out the milk, leaving the oat pulp behind. This will take a good 3 or 4 minutes. Alternatively, you could just pour the milk into a large bowl through a fine-mesh sieve, pressing down on the pulp with a spatula.

Pour the milk into a clean glass bottle or a large jar with a screw-top lid and store in the fridge for up to three days.

CASHEW MILK

MAKES 500ML

100g raw cashews

500ml filtered water

1 vanilla pod, split in half lengthways, seeds scraped out and pod discarded

1 tbsp honey or maple syrup

VEGAN if you use maple syrup

Put the cashews in a small bowl, cover them with water and cover the bowl with cling film. Let them soak overnight. The next day, drain the nuts and rinse them well.

Put the drained cashews in a powerful blender with the filtered water. Blend on high speed for 1–2 minutes, until the water turns white with little or no trace of cashews, which will be like fine crumbs. Add the vanilla seeds and sweetener and blitz again for a few seconds just to combine.

Line a large bowl with a clean nut milk bag or cheesecloth and pour the cashew milk into the cloth. Gather up the cloth, twist the top and use your hands to squeeze out the milk, leaving the pulp behind. This will take a good 3 or 4 minutes. Alternatively, you could just pour the milk into a large bowl through a fine-mesh sieve, pressing down on the pulp with a spatula.

Pour the milk into a clean glass bottle or a large jar with a screw-top lid and store in the fridge for up to three days.

ALMOND AND HAZELNUT MILK

MAKES 750ML

80g raw almonds

75g raw hazelnuts

750ml filtered water

1 vanilla pod, split in half lengthways, seeds scraped out and pod discarded

2 tbsp honey or maple syrup

pinch of sea salt

VEGAN if you use maple syrup

Put the nuts in a small bowl, cover them with water and cover the bowl with cling film. Let them soak overnight. The next day, drain the nuts and rinse them well.

Put the drained nuts in a powerful blender with the filtered water. Blend on high speed for 1 minute or so, until the water has turned white and the nuts are almost milled.

Line a large bowl with a clean nut milk bag or cheesecloth and pour the milk into the cloth. Gather up the cloth, twist the top and use your hands to squeeze out the milk, leaving the pulp behind. This will take a good 3 or 4 minutes. Alternatively, you could just pour the milk into a large bowl through a fine-mesh sieve, pressing down on the pulp with a spatula.

Give the blender a quick rinse, then pour the milk back in and add the vanilla seeds, sweetener and a pinch of sea salt and blitz again for a few seconds, just to combine. Pour the milk into a clean glass bottle or a large jar with a screw-top lid and store in the fridge for up to three days.

COCKTAILS

The key to maintaining a healthy lifestyle is balance. You can have a balanced diet and still enjoy an occasional drink or cocktail – with a healthy twist, of course! But cocktails aren't like cake. Just because they're healthy doesn't mean you can have more!

SAINTLY MOJITO

Instead of shaking and straining, I sometimes blend everything in a food processor and strain it through a sieve for an extreme mojito experience! **SERVES 1**

1 lime, unpeeled and cut into segments
....

handful of fresh mint leaves, chopped, plus an extra sprig to garnish
....

½ tbsp honey or maple syrup
....

50ml white rum
....

50ml coconut water
....

handful of crushed ice, plus extra to serve
....

Put the lime segments and mint leaves into a cocktail shaker and crush them together with a pestle or a muddler.

Zap the honey or maple syrup in the microwave to warm it up a little. Add it to the shaker along with the rest of the ingredients, put on the lid and shake well to combine.

Fill a glass (or an old jam jar if you want to be trendy) with ice. Strain the mojito into the glass and garnish with a sprig of fresh mint.

VEGAN if you use maple syrup

GLUTEN FREE depending on the brand of alcohol

MR PERFECT

SERVES 3

3 limes, peeled
....
1 cucumber
....
3 tbsp honey or maple
syrup
....
pinch of sea salt
....
750ml sparkling water
....
100ml vodka
....
4 lemon balm leaves or
fresh mint leaves
....
ice cubes, to serve
....

GLUTEN FREE depending
on the brand of alcohol

VEGAN if you use maple syrup

Juice the limes and cucumber, then whizz the juice with the honey and a pinch of sea salt in a blender until completely mixed. Pour into a pitcher and stir in the sparkling water, vodka and lemon balm or mint. Serve over ice.

PINK FLAMINGO

SERVES 2

50ml honey or maple syrup

50ml water

60ml vodka or gin

juice of 1 pink grapefruit

juice of ½ lemon

pinch of sea salt

ice cubes, to serve

G V D

GLUTEN FREE depending on the brand of alcohol

VEGAN if you use maple syrup

Bring the honey and water to a steady simmer in a small saucepan, until the honey has completely dissolved in the water. Remove from the heat and let this cool fully before combining with the vodka, grapefruit juice, lemon juice and a pinch of sea salt. Serve over ice.

PLAY IT COOL

SERVES 2

1 mango, peeled, chopped and frozen

2 Medjool dates, pitted

250ml freshly squeezed orange juice

125ml coconut water

50ml dark rum

3 tbsp desiccated coconut

crushed ice, to serve

fresh mint, to garnish

Put all the ingredients except the ice and mint into a high-speed blender and blitz until smooth. Pour into glasses over crushed ice and garnish with a sprig of fresh mint to serve.

GLUTEN FREE depending on the brand of alcohol

048

034

065

So many of us just rush through breakfast, but it can be one of the most creative meals of the day and it can really start your day on a high. Whether I'm on the go or having a lazy lie-in, I never miss my favourite meal.

BREAKFAST AND BRUNCH

COCONUT AND RASPBERRY 'PROATS'

Oats are the original fuel and are one of my top foods. But let's be honest – porridge gets boring, so I'm constantly trying to find new ways to make it taste and even look more appealing. Start with baked proats. It's the perfect way to trick yourself into enjoying oats. And don't worry, the egg whites won't make it taste eggy. They give it a natural lift and a creamy texture with a nice bit of protein to start the day, but if you don't have time to whisk the egg whites, add 1 teaspoon of baking powder and stir in the egg whites just as they are, without whisking them. **SERVES 1**

45g gluten-free oats

250ml coconut milk

1 tbsp desiccated coconut

2 egg whites

60g fresh raspberries

1 tsp honey or maple syrup

Preheat the oven to 190°C.

Place the oats and coconut milk into a small saucepan over a low heat. Cook, stirring, until it's a creamy porridge consistency that's a little on the stodgy side, then remove from the heat and stir in the desiccated coconut.

While the porridge is cooking, put the egg whites into a spotlessly clean, dry bowl and whisk until stiff peaks form. Stir the egg whites into the oats quickly so they don't start to cook, then stir in the raspberries and honey. Transfer to a baking dish and bake for 25 minutes, until browned on top.

SPICED APPLE AND WALNUT 'PROATS'

I always add whipped egg whites to my porridge, even if I'm not baking it. Use a fork to lightly whisk two egg whites in a bowl (they don't need to be stiff), then stir it into the porridge to make it extra creamy. **SERVES 1**

1 apple

45g gluten-free oats

250ml unsweetened almond milk

1 tbsp chia seeds (optional)

1 tsp ground cinnamon

1 tsp honey or maple syrup

2 egg whites

handful of walnut halves

Preheat the oven to 190°C.

Cut the apple in half. Grate one half and cut the other half into slices.

Place the oats and almond milk into a small saucepan over a low heat. Cook, stirring, until it's a thick, creamy porridge consistency that's a little on the stodgy side, then remove from the heat and stir in the grated apple, chia seeds, cinnamon and honey.

While the porridge is cooking, put the egg whites into a spotlessly clean, dry bowl and whisk until stiff peaks form. Stir the egg whites into the porridge quickly so they don't start to cook. Transfer to a baking dish and top with the apple slices and walnuts. Bake for 25 minutes, until browned on top.

CACAO AND ORANGE 'PROATS'

If you like to start the day with something sweet, then this is the breakfast for you. It's also really comforting as a quick supper after a long, cold day. Oats don't have to just be for breakfast! **SERVES 1**

1 tsp raw cacao powder

250ml unsweetened almond milk

45g gluten-free oats

zest of ½ orange

2 tbsp chopped nuts

1 tbsp honey or maple syrup

2 egg whites

G D

Preheat the oven to 190°C. Place the cacao powder in a small mixing bowl. Add a little almond milk and whisk together to make a paste, then add the rest of the milk and whisk to make a smooth chocolate milk, making sure there are no lumps.

Place the oats and chocolate milk into a small saucepan over a low heat. Cook, stirring, until it's a thick, creamy porridge consistency that's a little on the stodgy side, then remove from the heat and stir in the orange zest, nuts and honey.

While the porridge is cooking, put the egg whites into a spotlessly clean, dry bowl and whisk until stiff peaks form. Stir the egg whites into the porridge quickly so they don't start to cook. Transfer to a baking dish and bake for 25 minutes, until browned on top.

BANANA BREAD 'PROATS'

This tastes just like banana bread and is a nice change from your regular bowl of porridge. **SERVES 1**

1 banana
....

45g gluten-free oats
....

250ml unsweetened almond milk
....

3 tbsp chopped walnuts
....

1–2 tbsp honey or maple syrup
....

½ tsp ground cinnamon
....

½ tsp ground nutmeg
....

2 egg whites
....

G **D**

Preheat the oven to 190°C.

Start by mashing three-quarters of the banana and slicing the remaining quarter.

Place the oats and almond milk into a small saucepan over a low heat. Cook, stirring, until it's a thick, creamy porridge consistency that's a little on the stodgy side, then remove from the heat and stir in the mashed banana, walnuts, honey and spices.

While the porridge is cooking, put the egg whites into a spotlessly clean, dry bowl and whisk until stiff peaks form. Stir the egg whites into the porridge quickly so they don't start to cook. Transfer to a baking dish and top with the banana slices. Bake for 25 minutes, until browned on top.

CORN PORRIDGE

I first had creamed corn when I was in LA a few years ago and I polished off two bowls over dinner. After that, I started incorporating corn into desserts and other recipes where you wouldn't expect to find it – like porridge. Nothing beats fresh corn on the cob, so put down that tin! **SERVES 1**

1 ear of fresh corn on the cob

½ banana

50ml coconut milk

1 tsp ground cinnamon

35g gluten-free porridge oats

1 tsp stevia

Cut the corn kernels off the cob using a sharp knife. Place most of the corn in a food processor along with the banana, coconut milk and cinnamon and blend until you have a smooth yellow batter, then stir in the oats.

Place in a saucepan over a low heat and cook, stirring constantly, until it thickens and warms through. This should only take 3–4 minutes. If the porridge is getting too stodgy, add a little more coconut milk.

Serve with the reserved corn kernels and a sprinkling of stevia or your preferred sweetener on top.

COCONUT RICE PORRIDGE WITH QUICK CHIA JAM

Porridge doesn't always have to mean oats! If you're fond of rice pudding, you'll love this breakfast option, which is made just like regular oats. It reminds me of my granny's creamy rice pudding and is the perfect fuel if you have a long day ahead. **SERVES 1**

45g brown or white rice flakes
....

200ml coconut milk
....

quick blueberry chia jam (page 305), to serve
....

desiccated coconut, toasted buckwheat groats or nuts, to serve
....

Place the rice flakes and coconut milk in a saucepan. Bring to a boil, then reduce the heat and simmer for 5–6 minutes, until you reach your desired porridge consistency. Spoon into a bowl and serve with a dollop of chia jam and some desiccated coconut, toasted buckwheat groats or nuts scattered on top.

OATS ON THE GO

COCONUT AND GOJI BERRY OVERNIGHT OATS

If you have an early start in the morning, make one of these the night before and put it in a screw-top jar to get an extra few minutes in bed. Then all you need to do in the morning is throw the jar in your bag if you need to dash out the door and eat on the run. This one is my favourite combination. It's helped get me through some of my earliest call times. **SERVES 1**

45g gluten-free oats

250ml coconut water

2 tbsp goji berries

1 tbsp flaxseeds

Place all the ingredients in a jar and stir to combine. Screw on the lid and refrigerate overnight. The next morning, just give the oats a quick stir before tucking in.

COCONUT AND RAISIN OVERNIGHT OATS

SERVES 1

45g gluten-free oats

250ml coconut milk

2 tbsp raisins

2 tbsp desiccated coconut

½ tbsp honey or maple syrup

Place all the ingredients in a jar and stir to combine. Screw on the lid and refrigerate overnight.

VEGAN if you use maple syrup

CACAO AND DATE OVERNIGHT OATS

SERVES 1

1 tsp raw cacao powder

250ml unsweetened almond milk

45g gluten-free oats

2 dates, pitted and chopped

1 tbsp cacao nibs

1 tbsp honey or maple syrup

Place the cacao powder in a bowl. Add a little almond milk and whisk together to make a paste, then add the rest of the milk and whisk to make a smooth chocolate milk, making sure there are no lumps. Stir in the rest of the ingredients. Transfer to a jar, screw on the lid and refrigerate overnight.

VEGAN if you use maple syrup

GRANOLA WITH A TWIST

QUINOA BUCKWHEAT POPS

Out of all the breakfasts I make, this one lasts the shortest amount of time. Not only is it a great breakfast, but it's also an ideal snack. It's easy to make in bulk too – stored in a glass jar or airtight container, it will keep for up to two weeks. **MAKES 8 SERVINGS**

GRANOLA BASE:

200g buckwheat groats

130g raw nuts (I use hazelnuts and almonds)

80g quinoa pops or 160g quinoa flakes

80g sunflower seeds

2 star anise (optional)

1 tbsp ground cinnamon

1 tsp ground nutmeg

4 tbsp honey or maple syrup

1 tbsp vanilla essence

TOPPINGS:

3 tbsp goji berries

3 tbsp raw mulberries

2 tbsp cacao nibs

2 tbsp chia seeds

1 tbsp bee pollen

seasonal fruit compote (page 052), to serve

Preheat the oven to 170°C.

Mix all the dry ingredients together in a large mixing bowl. Gently warm the honey and vanilla, then pour it over and stir it in well.

Spread the granola out on a baking tray in an even layer. Bake for 35–40 minutes, stirring the granola every 10 minutes, until it's golden brown all over. Let it cool, then remove the star anise and stir in the toppings. Store in a glass jar or airtight container for up to two weeks and serve with seasonal fruit compote.

VEGAN if you use maple syrup and leave out the bee pollen

QUINOLA WITH CARAMELISED BANANA AND CASHEW CREAM

I know what you're thinking – what the hell is quinola? It's my made-up word for this simple granola made with quinoa. I have always made my own granola because more often than not, shop-bought ones are full of hidden sugars. You might think the cashew cream is too much effort, but I promise that it's worth it. If you're like me and crave cereal with ice-cold milk and a sweet crunch, then look no further than this recipe. Any leftover quinola is a great snack with some yoghurt. My favourite quinola combo is cacao nibs, goji berries, chopped almonds, finely chopped dates and mulberries. The mulberries are a must for me – they're like chewy bits of caramel. All these ingredients are always in my press anyway, but check what's in yours to see what you can work with. **SERVES 2**

QUINOLA:

2 tbsp coconut, almond or rapeseed oil

1 tsp honey or maple syrup

1 tsp vanilla essence

1 tsp ground cinnamon

½ tsp ground nutmeg

½ tsp ground ginger

80g quinoa flakes

3 tbsp flaxseeds

handful of chopped nuts and/ or seeds (optional)

3 tbsp chopped dried fruit (optional)

pinch of sea salt

QUINOLA EXTRAS:

desiccated coconut

cacao nibs

goji berries

mulberries

dried dates

dried apricots

chia seeds

CARAMELISED BANANA:

1 tsp coconut oil

½ small banana, peeled and sliced down the middle

1 tbsp freshly squeezed lemon juice

2 tsp coconut sugar

1 tsp ground cinnamon

cashew cream (page 307), to serve

non-dairy milk, to serve

VEGAN if you use maple syrup

Preheat the oven to 190°C.

Melt the oil, honey and vanilla together in a large bowl in the microwave for about 30 seconds. Stir in the cinnamon, nutmeg and ginger, then add the quinoa flakes and the flaxseeds and mix well. If you're using chopped nuts or seeds, stir them in now too.

Spread the mix out on a baking tray. Bake for 6–10 minutes, keeping a close eye on it. Shake the tray every few minutes to make sure it all gets toasted nicely. When the flakes look golden brown, remove the tray from the oven and let it cool. Add your chopped dried fruit or any other extras you like. Don't forget a pinch of sea salt!

Meanwhile, to make the caramelised banana, melt the oil in a frying pan over a medium heat. Add the sliced banana, cut side down, and don't stir or move it – let it get a nice golden colour. This will take about 40 seconds. Using a spatula, carefully turn the slices over and sprinkle over the lemon juice, coconut sugar and cinnamon. Cook for 1 minute, moving the bananas around a bit using the spatula, and turn them over once more.

Serve the quinola with the caramelised bananas and a dollop of cashew cream on top and pour in some ice-cold non-dairy milk.

FRUIT

BREAKFAST CRUMBLE

Leave it to me to make a dessert into breakfast, right? This is for a cold morning when you get to lie in and relax – the ultimate bowl of happiness. **SERVES 1**

½ tsp coconut oil

1 apple, sliced

2 handfuls of fresh berries

4 tbsp freshly squeezed orange juice

2 tbsp freshly squeezed lemon juice

1 tsp ground cinnamon

1 tsp honey or maple syrup (optional)

TOPPING:

50g chopped almonds

50g flaked almonds

25g quinoa or oat flakes

1 tbsp honey or maple syrup, warmed

1 tbsp melted coconut oil or butter

PALEO if you leave out the quinoa or oat flakes

VEGAN if you use maple syrup and coconut oil

Preheat the oven to 190°C.

Melt the coconut oil in a small saucepan over a medium heat, then sauté the apples for 4–5 minutes, until golden. Remove from the heat and stir in the berries, orange juice, lemon juice, cinnamon and honey (if using). Pour into a small ovenproof dish.

Put all the crumble ingredients in a bowl and mix them together using your hands, until the nuts and flakes are evenly coated in the warmed honey and melted oil.

Sprinkle the crumble topping over the apple mixture in the dish. Bake for 25 minutes, until it's golden and toasted. Don't eat it right away, though – it will be piping hot!

SEASONAL FRUIT COMPOTE

This recipe is a nice way to use up whatever ripe fruit you have and it goes great with just about everything, from pancakes to porridge, granola and even the cashew cream on page 307. **SERVES 2**

250g frozen berries

2 pieces of in-season fruit, such as plums, pears, apples or peaches, sliced

1 tbsp freshly squeezed lemon juice

1 tsp honey or maple syrup

1 vanilla pod, split in half lengthways, seeds scraped out and pod discarded

½ tsp orange zest (optional)

VEGAN if you use maple syrup

Place the berries and fruit in a medium-sized saucepan and bring to the boil, then reduce the heat and add the lemon juice and honey. Gently simmer for 15–20 minutes, until the fruit has broken down and thickened, stirring occasionally. Stir in the vanilla and orange zest, then remove the pan from the heat and let it sit with the lid on for 5 minutes before serving. Store the cooled compote in a glass jar in the fridge for up to two days.

PANCAKES AND CRÊPES

HAPPY QUINOA CRÊPES

I highly recommend purchasing a good non-stick frying pan as part of your kitchen kit. Nothing gets your day off to a bad start like a broken crêpe! These crêpes are the perfect use for quinoa. They're the result of a recipe collaboration with my two favourite foodies, Stephen and Dave from the Happy Pear in Greystones, Co. Wicklow. Check them out! **SERVES 2**

125g quinoa

2 tbsp flaxseeds

1 small banana, peeled

250ml rice milk

1 tsp vanilla essence

1 tbsp honey or maple syrup, plus extra to serve

pinch of sea salt

coconut oil, for frying

fresh berries, to serve

Put the uncooked quinoa and flaxseeds into a food processor and blend to form a flour. Add the rest of the ingredients except the oil and berries and blend again to form a batter.

Melt a little coconut oil in a non-stick frying pan over a high heat. Pour in half a cup of batter and spread it evenly over the base by tilting the pan. Reduce the heat to medium and cook for about 3 minutes on each side, until the edges start to lift up from the base of the pan. Repeat with the remaining batter.

Serve warm with a drizzle of honey or maple syrup and fresh berries.

VEGAN if you use maple syrup

OAT CRÊPES

I love taking old-fashioned breakfast ingredients like oats and making them into something that tastes like a treat. **SERVES 1**

50g gluten-free oats

2 eggs

2 tbsp non-dairy milk

1 ½ tbsp Greek yoghurt

1 tsp honey or maple syrup

coconut oil, for frying

chocolate pecan spread (page 315), to serve

sliced bananas, to serve

Blend the oats, eggs, milk, yoghurt and honey in a food processor until a smooth, thin batter forms.

Heat a little coconut oil in a non-stick frying pan over a high heat. Pour in one-third of the batter and spread it evenly over the base by tilting the pan or by using the back of a spoon. Immediately reduce the heat to low and cook for about 2 minutes, until bubbles start to appear on top and the edges begin to lift up from the base of the pan.

Flip the crêpe over and cook for 1 minute more, until golden brown. Repeat with the remaining batter, making sure you always start off with a high heat and then reduce it as soon as you pour in the batter so that the crêpes all cook evenly.

Serve warm with a little chocolate pecan spread and sliced bananas.

PROTEIN CRÊPES

I feel like Rocky when I wake up and make this breakfast – it's an extreme protein hit! I love serving these with lemon and stevia, as it tastes like proper traditional crêpes.

SERVES 1

2 eggs

2 egg whites

1 scoop (30g) vanilla whey protein powder

2 tbsp non-dairy milk

1 tsp coconut oil

squeeze of lemon, to serve

pinch of stevia, to serve

Greek yoghurt, to serve (optional)

GLUTEN FREE depending on whey protein powder

Blend the eggs, egg whites, protein powder and milk in a food processor until a smooth, thin batter forms.

Melt the coconut oil in a non-stick frying pan over a high heat. Reduce the heat to medium, then pour in one-third of the batter and spread it evenly over the base by tilting the pan. Cook for 2–3 minutes on each side, until lightly browned. Repeat with the remaining batter.

Serve warm with a squeeze of lemon and a sprinkle of stevia or a dollop of Greek yoghurt.

SPICED APPLE PANCAKES

Coconut flour can be difficult to work with, so make sure you follow the guidelines and use your batter as soon as you make it, as it can dry out quickly. The consistency of this batter is a little thicker than usual due to the coconut flour, but it gives these pancakes a lovely crumpet-style texture. **MAKES 3 PANCAKES**

30g coconut flour
....

1 tsp stevia
....

1 tsp ground cinnamon
....

2 egg whites
....

1 egg
....

80ml unsweetened
almond milk
....

1 tsp vanilla essence
....

1 small apple, grated
....

coconut oil, for frying
....

TOPPING:

1 small apple, finely sliced
....

1½ tsp ground cinnamon
....

Place the coconut flour, stevia and cinnamon in a large bowl and mix together.

In a separate bowl, whisk together the egg whites, whole egg, almond milk and vanilla essence. Add this to the dry ingredients and mix until it's just combined and smooth – don't over mix. Fold in the grated apple.

Heat a little coconut oil in a non-stick frying pan over a high heat. Spoon in 3 tablespoons of the batter at a time and smooth it out with the back of the spoon. Cook for 2–3 minutes, until the base is set. Lower the heat to medium, then flip it over and cook for a further 3 minutes, until cooked through. Repeat with the remaining batter and keep the pancakes warm.

To make the topping, place the frying pan back on a high heat and melt a little more coconut oil. Toss in the apple slices, then lower the heat to medium. Cook, stirring constantly, for 3–4 minutes, until the apples start to soften (this will depend on how thick you sliced them). Sprinkle over the cinnamon and remove from the heat.

Put the pancakes on a plate and serve with the sautéed apples spooned on top.

SAVOURY BUCKWHEAT CRÊPES WITH CREAMY MUSHROOMS AND SPINACH

Believe it or not, I do sometimes eat savoury breakfasts too. These super versatile crêpes can be filled with whatever is in your fridge, but my favourite filling is sliced ham, crumbled feta cheese and the fiery relish on page 299. They also keep well if you make them the night before and fill them in the morning. **SERVES 2**

170g buckwheat flour
....
2 tbsp milled flaxseeds
....
1 tbsp dried herbs
....
1 tsp sea salt
....
500ml water
....
rapeseed or coconut oil,
for frying
....
100g button or chestnut
mushrooms, sliced
....
creamed spinach (page 111)
....

Put the buckwheat flour in a large mixing bowl. Using a fork, whisk in the milled flaxseeds, the dried herbs, the salt and 375ml of the water. Let the batter sit in the fridge for 20 minutes, then stir in the remaining 125ml of water.

Heat a little oil in a non-stick frying pan over a high heat. Reduce the heat to medium, then pour in ½ cup of batter and spread it evenly over the base by tilting the pan. Cook for 1–2 minutes, until it's almost cooked through, then flip over and cook for 1 minute more. Transfer to a plate and set aside and repeat with the remaining batter.

In a separate pan, heat a little more oil and gently cook the mushrooms for about 4 minutes, until soft. Add the creamed spinach and cook, stirring, for 1 minute more.

Spoon the filling onto the crêpe and fold it in half or quarters to serve.

OAT PANCAKES WITH SWEET PEANUT SAUCE

I won't lie, I eat these every second morning but I never get tired of them. These pancakes work well with every sort of topping and sometimes I throw a scoop of protein powder into the mix to shake things up a little. I usually make a huge batch and store it in the fridge. One of the worst mistakes I made was teaching my boyfriend how to make these – it's all he eats now and pancake batter is always everywhere! My secret for consistent, perfect pancakes is to use egg moulds. **MAKES 4 SMALL PANCAKES**

OAT PANCAKES:

50g gluten-free oats
....

1 scoop (30g) protein powder (optional)
....

1 egg
....

1½ tbsp Greek yoghurt, plus extra to serve
....

1 tsp honey or maple syrup
....

½ tsp gluten-free baking powder
....

coconut oil, for frying
....

SWEET PEANUT SAUCE:

1 tbsp coconut oil
....

1 tsp honey or maple syrup
....

1 tbsp peanut butter
....

To make the sweet peanut sauce, just melt the coconut oil with the honey in a small saucepan over a low heat, then stir in the peanut butter until it makes a smooth sauce. Set aside while you make the pancakes.

To make the oat pancakes, blend all the ingredients except the oil in a food processor until smooth. I use my NutriBullet for this.

Heat a little coconut oil in a non-stick frying pan, then wipe it out with kitchen paper. Add spoonfuls of the batter to the pan – it's a thick batter, so make small pancakes. Cook for 2 minutes, until the bottom is golden brown and ready to be turned. Flip over and cook for 1–2 minutes more, until golden brown. Repeat with the remaining batter. Serve warm with a drizzle of sweet peanut sauce or a dollop of Greek yoghurt.

CHOCOLATE BERRY PANCAKES

Berries and chocolate are a perfect combination for a breakfast favourite – the pancake stack! Paired with this quick berry sauce and creamy Greek yoghurt, you would never guess it's 100% healthy. **SERVES 1**

3 heaped tbsp coconut flour

3 tsp stevia

1 tsp raw cacao powder

1 tsp raw carob or cacao powder

½ tsp gluten-free baking powder

2 eggs

2 egg whites

80ml coconut milk

1 tsp vanilla essence

375g berries (I use raspberries and blueberries)

coconut oil, for frying

4 tbsp Greek yoghurt or dairy-free yoghurt, to serve (optional)

DAIRY FREE if you use non-dairy yoghurt

Place the coconut flour, 2 teaspoons of the stevia, the cacao powder, carob powder and baking powder in a large bowl and mix together.

In a separate bowl, whisk together the whole eggs, egg whites, coconut milk and vanilla. Using a fork, mix this into the dry ingredients until a smooth batter forms. Cut 100g of the berries in half and stir them into the batter.

Melt a little coconut oil in a non-stick frying pan over a high heat. Spoon in 3 tablespoons of the batter at a time and smooth it out with the back of the spoon, then immediately reduce the heat to medium. Cook for 4–5 minutes, until the base is set. Flip it over and cook for a further 4–5 minutes, until cooked through. Repeat with the remaining batter.

To make the berry sauce, place the rest of the berries in a bowl and microwave on high for 2 minutes, checking them after the first minute and stirring. Add the remaining teaspoon of stevia and mix using a fork.

To serve, place one pancake on a plate and add a spoonful of the berry sauce and a tablespoon of Greek yoghurt on top. Continue layering with more pancakes, berry sauce and yoghurt, finishing with some berry sauce poured over the stack.

SAVOURY OATCAKES WITH SMOKED SALMON AND HERB MAYO

I love smoked salmon for breakfast but I also love my oat crêpes, so I just put them together to create a simple, savoury duo of two of my favourite things. **SERVES 1**

50g gluten-free oats

1 egg

1 ½ tbsp Greek yoghurt

2 tsp mixed dried herbs

1 tsp sea salt

½ tsp gluten-free baking powder

rapeseed oil, for frying

3 tbsp homemade mayo (page 300)

40g smoked salmon

Put the oats in a food processor and blend into a fine flour. Add the egg, yoghurt, 1 teaspoon of the dried herbs, the salt and the baking powder and blend until smooth.

Heat a little oil in a non-stick frying pan, then wipe it away with a piece of kitchen paper. Add in spoonfuls of the batter – it will be thick, so aim to make about four small crumpet-style pancakes. Cook for 2 minutes, until the base is golden brown and ready to be turned. Flip over and cook for 1 minute more, until golden brown. Repeat with the remaining batter, adding a little oil to the pan and wiping it out each time.

To make the herb mayo, put the mayo and the remaining teaspoon of dried herbs in a small bowl and stir to combine.

To serve, place the oatcakes on a plate and drape the smoked salmon over them. Finish with a dollop of the herb mayo.

EGGS

MACKEREL SALAD WITH PAPRIKA 'MAYO' STUFFED EGGS

I never get tired of eggs, but if you're sick of using the same recipes over and over again, it's time to broaden your egg repertoire and bring back the egg love. Get cracking! You can replace the mackerel with tuna or even some torn slices of Serrano ham. **SERVES 1**

2 eggs

½ **ripe avocado, peeled and stoned**

1 tbsp freshly squeezed lemon juice

1 tbsp chopped fresh coriander leaves

½ **tsp smoked paprika, plus extra to garnish**

½ **tsp Dijon mustard**

handful of rocket leaves

55g smoked mackerel

lemon slice, to garnish

Place the eggs in a saucepan and add enough cold water to cover the eggs by 2.5cm. Bring to the boil, then remove from the heat, cover the pan and let them sit in the hot water for 12 minutes. Remove the eggs from the water with a slotted spoon and run under cold water to cool them down.

Once the eggs are cool enough to handle, peel them and cut them in half lengthways, removing the yolks. Place the hardboiled yolks, avocado, lemon juice, coriander, smoked paprika and mustard in a food processor and blend together.

Use a small spoon to fill the hollowed-out egg whites with the 'mayo'. There will be some left over, so use this to garnish the mackerel salad. Sprinkle the eggs with a little smoked paprika.

To finish the salad, place the rocket leaves on a plate and flake over the mackerel. Nestle the filled eggs into the rocket and add dollops of the remaining 'mayo' to serve. Garnish with a lemon slice.

EGG WRAPS WITH SMOKED MACKEREL AND SPINACH

These are a handy alternative to traditional lunchtime wraps. **SERVES 1**

2 eggs

2 egg whites

1 tbsp milled flaxseeds

sea salt and freshly ground black pepper

coconut oil, for frying

FILLING:

½ ripe avocado, peeled, stoned and mashed

60g smoked mackerel, flaked into bite-sized pieces

handful of baby spinach

homemade fiery relish (page 299)

Place the eggs, egg whites, milled flaxseeds and some salt and pepper in a blender and whizz for 1 minute.

Heat a little oil in a non-stick frying pan over a high heat. Reduce the heat to medium and pour in the eggy batter, spreading it evenly over the base by tilting the pan. Cook for 2–3 minutes on each side, until set and cooked through.

Transfer the wrap to a cutting board. Spread with the mashed avocado, then scatter the smoked mackerel and baby spinach on top and finish with a few small dollops of relish. Roll up tightly and cut in half on the diagonal to serve.

MACKEREL AND POACHED EGGS WITH HEALTHY HOLLANDAISE

I'm a bit of a hollandaise fiend. I even have a hollandaise ranking of Dublin brunch spots. The real deal is a nice treat now and again if I go out for breakfast, but this healthier version hits the spot if I'm having a friend over for brunch at home. **SERVES 2**

a few drops of vinegar
(I use apple cider vinegar)
....

4 very fresh eggs
....

rapeseed oil, for frying
....

2 fresh mackerel fillets
....

HEALTHY HOLLANDAISE:

2 egg yolks
....

1 tbsp freshly squeezed
lemon juice
....

2 tsp nutritional yeast
....

3 tbsp coconut oil, melted
and piping hot
....

2 tbsp chopped fresh dill
....

pinch of sea salt
....

pinch of cayenne pepper
(optional)
....

Fresh eggs are the key to perfect poached eggs. Fill a saucepan until the water is about 10cm deep and bring to a steady simmer, then add a drop of vinegar. Crack each egg into a separate small cup. Create a whirlpool in the saucepan with a slotted spoon and gently slide one egg at a time into the centre. Cook for 3 minutes. Gently lift out with a slotted spoon and set aside to drain on a plate lined with kitchen paper while you cook the mackerel.

Heat a drop of oil in a skillet over a medium-high heat, then add the mackerel, skin side up. Cook for 2–3 minutes, until the sides are beginning to brown. Carefully flip over using a fish slice or spatula and cook the other side for 2–3 minutes more, until the fish is cooked through. Keep the fish warm while you make the hollandaise.

To make the hollandaise sauce, whisk together the egg yolks, lemon juice and nutritional yeast in a large bowl until well combined. Melt the coconut oil in a small saucepan over a high heat – you need it to be piping hot. Slowly add the hot oil to the egg yolks a little bit at a time, whisking continuously. Alternatively, you can make this in a blender on a low speed. The egg yolks will immediately turn pale and start to thicken. Once all the oil has been incorporated, stir in the dill, a pinch of salt and cayenne pepper, if using. Use the sauce straight away, as hollandaise doesn't like to sit around.

Transfer the mackerel to a serving plate. Gently place the poached eggs on top, then drizzle over the hollandaise.

DUCK EGG FRITTATA WITH SPINACH AND SWEET POTATO

I discovered duck eggs about four years ago and it was love at first bite. The yolks are almost twice the size of hen's eggs and are full of rich fats and nutrients. **SERVES 3**

1 sweet potato, peeled and diced
....

4 duck eggs
....

2 egg whites (hen's eggs)
....

2 handfuls of baby spinach, chopped
....

25g feta or Parmesan cheese (optional)
....

sea salt and freshly ground black pepper
....

Preheat the oven to 190°C.

Steam the sweet potato for about 15 minutes, until soft.

Whisk the duck eggs and the regular egg whites in a mixing bowl, then stir in the spinach, cooked sweet potato, cheese and seasoning. Pour into a non-stick ovenproof frying pan or dish and bake in the oven for 15 minutes, until cooked through and set. Cut into wedges and serve warm or at room temperature.

G D

DAIRY FREE if you leave out the cheese

SPICY SWEET POTATO AND EGG BAKE

This is the perfect dish to make if you're having people around for breakfast or brunch, plus the sweet potato really satisfies a carbs craving. You could also use 50g cooked lentils instead of the sweet potatoes if you like. **SERVES 2**

2 tbsp rapeseed oil

½ red onion, chopped

1 sweet potato, peeled and cut into 1cm cubes

1 sweet red pepper, cut into cubes

1 fresh red chilli, deseeded and finely chopped

1 tsp paprika or cayenne pepper

400g ripe tomatoes, chopped

50ml water

sea salt and freshly ground black pepper

2 eggs

chopped fresh coriander, to garnish

chopped fresh flat-leaf parsley, to garnish

Preheat the oven to 200°C.

Heat the oil in a large ovenproof frying pan over a medium heat. Sauté the onion for 5 minutes, then add the sweet potato, red pepper, chilli and paprika and cook for 5 minutes more, until the potatoes begin to soften. Add the tomatoes and water and cook for a further 5 minutes, until slightly thickened, then season with salt and pepper.

Make two wells and crack in the eggs. Transfer the pan to the oven and cook for 7–10 minutes, until the eggs are cooked through. Garnish with fresh coriander and parsley and serve straight to the table to let everyone help themselves, but remember that the handle will still be hot! Wrap a tea towel around it so no one accidentally burns themselves.

074

077

079

SOUPS

Eating soup is a fantastic way to
load up on your vegetables and
keep warm during all the Irish
seasons! Soups are ideal for
making in bulk and all the soups
in this chapter freeze well, bar
the chicken noodle soup.

PARSNIP AND LEMONGRASS SOUP

This soup originated from a stash of lemongrass I didn't want to go to waste, and boy am I glad I did something with it because it's become my favourite soup. **SERVES 6**

3 large parsnips, diced

2 medium carrots, diced

coconut oil, for roasting and frying

2 tsp regular honey, manuka honey or maple syrup

sea salt and freshly ground black pepper

2 onions, chopped

3 garlic cloves, crushed

5cm piece of fresh root ginger, peeled and grated

2 stalks of fresh lemongrass

handful of fresh coriander leaves, roughly chopped

1 tsp ground cinnamon

750ml vegetable stock

4 kaffir lime leaves

1 x 400ml tin of coconut milk

Preheat the oven to 200°C.

Place the parsnips and carrots on a baking tray. Melt 1 tablespoon of coconut oil with the honey and drizzle it over the veg along with some salt and pepper. Roast for 25 minutes, until lightly golden and soft.

Meanwhile, melt a little more coconut oil in a large saucepan over a low heat. Sweat the onions, garlic and ginger for 8–10 minutes, until the onions are softened but not browned.

While they're cooking, remove the outer leaves from the lemongrass stalks and cut away the tough upper half and the base. Cut the stalks in half to reveal the tender core and dice this part. Stir in the diced lemongrass, coriander and cinnamon and cook for 3–4 minutes, until fragrant.

Add the vegetable stock along with the roasted parsnips and carrots and the kaffir lime leaves. Bring to the boil, then reduce the heat to low and let it simmer for 20 minutes. Remove the lime leaves, then blend the soup in a high-speed blender or directly in the pot with a hand-held blender until it's smooth and thick. Let it cool a little before whisking in the coconut milk until it's thoroughly combined.

VEGAN if you use maple syrup

SERENE GREEN SOUP

Pure green soups can be hard to stomach sometimes. This one is great for any veggie dodgers, as it's packed full of nutrients and is tasty as hell. **SERVES 6**

coconut oil, olive oil or
butter, for frying
....

1 large onion, chopped
....

3 garlic cloves, minced
....

25g fresh basil leaves
....

3 courgettes, chopped
....

250g baby spinach
....

1 litre vegetable stock
....

600g frozen peas
....

flaxseed oil, to garnish
(optional)
....

freshly ground black pepper
....

Heat a little oil or butter in a large saucepan over a medium heat. Sauté the onions and garlic for about 6 minutes, until the onions are translucent, then stir in the basil and cook for 1 minute more. Toss in the chopped courgettes and cook, stirring, for a further 6 minutes.

Add the spinach, then pour in the vegetable stock. Bring to the boil, then reduce the heat and let it simmer for 25 minutes over a low heat. Stir in the peas, raise the heat to medium and cook for a further 5 minutes. Blend until smooth. Ladle into bowls and drizzle with flaxseed oil, if using, to serve and grind some black pepper on top.

DAIRY FREE if you use
coconut or olive oil

VEGAN if you use coconut or
olive oil

CHILLI BEET SOUP

This soup has a fiery kick that will leave you bursting with energy – not for the faint hearted! **SERVES 6**

1.5kg beetroot, peeled and chopped
....

coconut oil, for roasting and frying
....

1 large red onion, chopped
....

2 stalks of celery, chopped
....

3 garlic cloves, chopped
....

1 tbsp chilli flakes, plus extra to garnish
....

1 tbsp ground cumin
....

50ml apple cider vinegar
....

2 litres vegetable stock
....

Greek yoghurt, to serve (optional)
....

DAIRY FREE, VEGAN AND PALEO if you leave out the yoghurt

Preheat the oven to 200°C.

Place the chopped beetroot on a baking tray and toss with a little coconut oil. Roast for 25 minutes, until tender.

Meanwhile, heat 2 tablespoons of coconut oil in a large saucepan over a low heat. Sweat the onion for 10 minutes with the lid on, stirring once, then add the roasted beetroot along with the celery, garlic, chilli flakes and cumin and cook for 10 minutes more, covered, until all the vegetables have softened. Pour in the vinegar and cook, stirring, for 4–5 minutes. Add the stock and let it simmer for 20 minutes on a medium-low heat. Blend until smooth and ladle into bowls. Garnish with a pinch of chilli flakes, or if you're not used to this much heat, serve the soup with a swirl of Greek yoghurt to tone down the kick!

ROAST CARROT AND RED PEPPER SOUP

Two of my favourite veg are teamed together in this soup, and both are great for your skin. **SERVES 6**

4 carrots, cut into quarters
....

4 sprigs of fresh thyme, leaves only
....

sea salt and freshly ground black pepper
....

rapeseed oil, for roasting and frying
....

4 red bell peppers, deseeded and halved
....

2 sweet red peppers, deseeded and halved
....

1 onion, chopped
....

2 stalks of celery, chopped
....

2 garlic cloves, chopped
....

1.2 litres vegetable stock
....

handful of fresh flat-leaf parsley, roughly chopped
....

1 bay leaf
....

flaxseed oil, to garnish
....

Preheat the oven to 200°C.

Place the carrots on a baking tray with two of the thyme sprigs. Season well and drizzle with a little rapeseed oil. Roast for 30–35 minutes, until browned a little. Place the halved peppers on a separate baking tray and roast them for 20 minutes.

Heat 2 tablespoons of rapeseed oil in a large saucepan over a low heat. Sweat the onion, celery and garlic for 15 minutes, until soft. Add the roasted carrots and peppers, vegetable stock, parsley, bay leaf and remaining thyme.

Simmer for 15 minutes, then remove the bay leaf and blend until smooth. Ladle into bowls and garnish with a drizzle of flaxseed oil.

CHICKEN NOODLE SOUP

The original flu fighter, this soup can even cure man flu. This soup does take a long time to cook, but nothing beats homemade chicken noodle soup made from scratch. The next time your better half is unwell, you have no excuse now – get your apron on! **SERVES 8**

3 tbsp dried sage

3 tbsp flaky sea salt

1 large whole chicken

500g carrots, chopped

2 large onions, chopped

2 heads of garlic, broken into cloves and chopped

5 bay leaves

1 tsp chilli powder

300g mung bean noodles, glass noodles or spiralised courgette or butternut squash

2 fresh ears of corn, cut off the cob

chopped fresh flat-leaf parsley, to garnish

lime wedges, to serve

Mix the dried sage and sea salt together in a small bowl, then rub the chicken all over with the herb salt. Place the chicken in a large pot with the carrots, onions, garlic, bay leaves and chilli powder and fill it up with enough water to just cover the chicken. Bring to a boil, then reduce the heat and simmer for 2 hours, uncovered, skimming off any foam that rises to the surface.

Remove the chicken and allow it to cool a little, then pull the meat off the bones and discard the skin. Place the noodles in the stock and cook them for 5–10 minutes, until soft, or according to the instructions on the packet. Place the shredded chicken back in the pot and add the corn kernels. Simmer on a low heat for 5 minutes, then discard the bay leaves, ladle the soup into bowls and garnish with chopped fresh parsley. Serve with lime wedges.

PALEO if you use vegetable noodles

CHICKEN RAMEN

This is my go-to dinner option when I want to trim up but still need something satisfying and filling. **SERVES 2**

2 chicken breasts

pinch of sea salt

1 tbsp toasted sesame oil

1 red onion, sliced into half moons

3 garlic cloves, minced

1 large carrot, cut into cubes

5cm piece of fresh root ginger, peeled and grated

700ml chicken stock

3 tbsp tamari

3 tbsp mirin

70g mung bean noodles, rice noodles or courgette noodles

30g baby spinach or kale, chopped

1 tbsp honey

snipped fresh chives, to garnish

Place the chicken breasts in a saucepan that will just about fit them and pour in enough water to fully cover the chicken. Sprinkle in a generous pinch of salt and bring the water to a boil, then reduce the heat, cover the pan with a lid and let it simmer for about 15 minutes. You can check that the chicken is cooked through by making an incision in the thickest part of the breast – there should be no traces of pink. Remove from the pan and pat dry with some kitchen paper, then slice thinly.

Heat the sesame oil in a large saucepan over a low heat. Sweat the onion and garlic for 8 minutes, then turn the heat up to medium, add the carrot and ginger and cook for 2–3 minutes more. Add the sliced chicken, then stir in the chicken stock, tamari and mirin. Add the noodles and spinach and cook for 3–5 minutes, until the noodles are soft. Finally, stir in the honey. Ladle the ramen into bowls and garnish with fresh snipped chives.

  G P D

PALEO if you use courgette noodles

CREAMY BACON AND MUSHROOM SOUP

A good, simple mushroom soup doesn't need lots of extras. Yet it can be hit or miss, particularly as it's usually made with lashings of cream and butter. You won't miss them in this version, I promise. **SERVES 6**

coconut oil, for frying

1 large onion, chopped

2 garlic cloves, chopped

750g mix of Portobello and button mushrooms, chopped

a few sprigs of fresh thyme, leaves only

handful of fresh flat-leaf parsley, chopped

1 litre vegetable stock

3 bacon rashers

1 x 400ml tin of full-fat coconut milk

VEGAN if you leave out the bacon topping

Melt 1 tablespoon of coconut oil in a large saucepan over a low heat. Sweat the onion and garlic for 8–10 minutes, until softened. Raise the heat to medium, add the chopped mushrooms and fresh herbs and cook for 10 minutes. Pour in the vegetable stock, reduce the heat back to low and simmer for 15–20 minutes.

While the soup is simmering, heat a frying pan over a medium heat. Add 1–2 teaspoons of oil and cook the bacon for a few minutes on each side, until it's crisp and golden. Set aside on a plate lined with kitchen paper to soak up the excess oil, then cut off the rind and dice the bacon into small pieces.

When the soup is done, blend until it's completely smooth. Pour the soup back into the saucepan and stir in the coconut milk. Heat gently for a few minutes to allow the coconut milk to warm through, then ladle the soup into bowls and garnish with the cooked diced bacon.

096

086

091

098

I'm not much of a fan of stereotypical salads. These are definitely more energising, comforting bowls that won't leave you feeling hungry or unsatisfied.

SALADS

Here's a little tip: any time you're cooking quinoa for another dish, make some extra or even make a double batch so that you can use the leftovers in salads. Or if you roast a whole chicken, shred the leftover meat and add some to salads for an extra protein hit.

QUINOA SALAD WITH BROCCOLI, FETA AND HAZELNUTS

This is my favourite salad. I like to make a big batch to have for lunch throughout the week – just keep the dressing separate. I sometimes add some shredded roast chicken for extra protein. I often make this salad during my cooking demos and it's always a big hit, especially the dressing, which I also use as a vegetable dip or to liven up plain dishes.

SERVES 4

260g quinoa

100g red split lentils

100g raw hazelnuts

50g mix of pumpkin and sunflower seeds

8 cherry tomatoes, halved

1 red onion, finely chopped

½ small head of broccoli, chopped

½ large cucumber, cut into cubes

75g feta cheese, cut into cubes

25g fresh flat-leaf parsley, chopped

DRESSING:

juice of 1 lemon

2 tbsp light tahini

2 tbsp apple cider vinegar

1 tbsp honey or maple syrup

1 level tbsp Dijon mustard

2 tsp tamari or soya sauce

1 tsp sea salt

Rinse the quinoa under cold running water to get rid of its bitter coating. Place the quinoa in a saucepan and pour in 750ml water. Cover the saucepan and bring to the boil, then reduce the heat and simmer for 15–20 minutes, until the germ has separated from the seed. Tip into a colander to drain off any excess water, then set aside and allow it to cool (I keep it covered while it's cooling, which helps it to fluff up).

Put the lentils and 250ml water into a separate small saucepan. Bring to a boil, then reduce the heat and simmer for 10 minutes, until the lentils have softened but haven't turned to mush. Remove from the heat, strain and set aside to cool completely.

To toast the hazelnuts, preheat the oven to 200°C. Put them on a baking tray and toast them in the oven for 10–15 minutes, until the skins have started to loosen. Remove the hazelnut skins using the roast-and-rub method: tip the warm nuts into a slightly dampened kitchen towel, fold up the sides and rub the skins off using the towel.

To toast the pumpkin and sunflower seeds, spread them over a baking tray and toast them in the oven along with the hazelnuts for a few minutes, until they start to turn golden. Tip the seeds out of the tray and set them aside.

When the quinoa and lentils are cool, place them in a large mixing bowl with the remaining salad ingredients, including the toasted hazelnuts and seeds. Use a fork to toss everything together.

In a separate small bowl, whisk together all the dressing ingredients until smooth. Drizzle most of the dressing over the salad and toss to combine. Divide the salad between shallow bowls or plates and drizzle the rest of the dressing on top.

QUINOA COMFORT BOWL

This salad is one of my favourite combinations of textures and flavours. It will keep you full for ages. **SERVES 2**

1 golden or regular beetroot, peeled and cut into bite-sized cubes
....
½ medium sweet potato, peeled and cut into bite-sized cubes
....
1 tbsp rapeseed oil
....
sea salt and freshly ground black pepper
....
15g shelled pistachio nuts
....
40g leftover cooked quinoa
....
2 small radishes, sliced
....
6 fresh mint leaves, shredded
....
¼ pomegranate, seeds only
....
juice of 1 lemon
....
1 tbsp olive oil
....
1 tsp ground cumin
....

Preheat the oven to 200°C. Line a baking tray with tin foil.

Place the beetroot and sweet potato cubes on the lined tray. Drizzle with the rapeseed oil and season with some salt and pepper. Cook for 35–40 minutes, until the vegetables are soft and golden. Let them cool a little before you add them to the other salad ingredients.

To toast the pistachios, reduce the oven temperature to 180°C. Spread out the nuts on a baking tray in a single layer. Put them in the oven for just a few minutes, until they start to brown. Tip the nuts out of the tray and set aside.

Combine the roasted beetroot and sweet potato with the cooked quinoa, radishes, mint, pomegranate seeds and toasted pistachios in a large mixing bowl. In a separate small bowl, whisk together the lemon juice, olive oil and cumin and drizzle this dressing over the salad, tossing to combine.

  G V D

PSYCHEDELIC SALAD

During the hotter months, I challenge myself to eat one raw meal a day. It definitely boosts my energy levels and pushes me to make dishes that taste and look the best they can. **SERVES 2**

50g frozen edamame beans
....

20g pumpkin seeds
....

2 carrots
....

1 courgette
....

1 beetroot, peeled
....

¼ head of red cabbage, cored and shredded
....

½ pomegranate, seeds only
....

1 ear of fresh corn on the cob
....

TAHINI DRESSING:

juice of 1 lemon
....

3 tbsp water
....

2 tbsp light tahini
....

2 tbsp apple cider vinegar
....

1 tsp cayenne pepper
....

pinch of sea salt
....

First cook the edamame beans. Bring a small pan of water to a boil. Add the edamame beans and boil them for 2–3 minutes to blanch them. Drain and refresh under cold running water to stop them cooking and to keep their bright green colour.

To toast the pumpkin seeds, heat a heavy-based, dry frying pan over a medium heat. Add the pumpkin seeds and cook, stirring, for 4–5 minutes, just until they start to turn golden. Tip the seeds out of the pan and set aside.

Using a spiraliser or julienne peeler, make vegetable noodles from the carrots, courgette and beetroot. Put the vegetable noodles in a large mixing bowl with the cooked edamame beans, toasted pumpkin seeds, shredded cabbage and pomegranate seeds.

Cut the corn off the cob using a sharp knife and add the raw kernels (yes, raw!) to the rest of the ingredients and mix everything together.

To make the tahini dressing, simply put all the ingredients into a mug or small bowl and whisk them together with a fork. Drizzle the salad with the tahini dressing and serve straight away.

SPINACH, AVOCADO AND ORANGE SALAD WITH CHICKPEA 'CROUTONS'

The perfect salad for your summer get-togethers. **SERVES 2**

100g baby spinach

2 oranges, peeled and segmented

1 ripe avocado, peeled, stoned and sliced

80g crunchy baked chickpeas (page 194)

DRESSING:

juice of ½ lemon

3 tbsp orange juice

2 tbsp extra virgin olive oil or nut oil

1 tsp ground cumin

sea salt and freshly ground black pepper

To make the dressing, simply whisk all the ingredients together.

Toss together the spinach leaves, orange segments and avocado in a bowl. Pour over the dressing and toss again to combine, then scatter over the chickpea 'croutons'.

TABBOULEH WITH AUBERGINE, AVOCADO AND POMEGRANATE

I love traditional tabbouleh, but I felt it needed to be taken up a notch. This version is an explosion of textures and flavours. **SERVES 2**

1 aubergine, sliced into 2cm-thick discs

20g flaked or whole almonds, toasted

100g bulgur wheat

300ml water

pinch of sea salt

½ ripe avocado, peeled, stoned and diced

¼ pomegranate, seeds only

15g fresh coriander, chopped

10g fresh mint leaves, shredded

3 tbsp raisins or dried cranberries

2 tbsp hemp seeds

juice of ½ lemon

1½ tbsp extra virgin olive oil

Preheat the oven to 200°C.

Place the aubergine slices on a baking tray and cook them in the oven for 35 minutes, until softened and browned. Allow to cool slightly.

Spread out the almonds on a separate baking tray and place in the oven for 10 minutes if you're using whole almonds or 4–5 minutes for flaked, tossing halfway through, until they are evenly browned. Set aside to cool.

Place the bulgur in a heatproof mixing bowl. Boil the water in a kettle, but only pour in just enough water to cover the bulgur. Stir in the salt, then cover the bowl with cling film and let it stand for 20 minutes. Drain off any excess water and put the bulgur in a large bowl, fluffing it up with a fork.

Mix all the remaining ingredients except the lemon juice and oil with the bulgur, including the cooled aubergine. Transfer to two wide, shallow bowls and serve with a drizzle of lemon juice and a good-quality olive oil.

SIMPLE WARM SALAD

This is a complete bowl of comfort, especially when you get home on a cold evening and you want something fast. **SERVES 1**

1 courgette, diced

1 tbsp extra virgin olive oil

2 tbsp freshly squeezed lemon juice

25g whole almonds, halved, or pine nuts

30g leftover cooked quinoa, reheated

1 tbsp vegan pesto (page 301)

2 tbsp dried cranberries

Roast the courgette in the oven or cook it on the hob. To roast it, preheat the oven to 180°C. Place the diced courgette on a baking tray, drizzle with a little oil and the lemon juice and cook for 35 minutes, until soft and browned along the edges. To cook it on the hob, heat the oil in a frying pan over a medium heat. Add the diced courgette and cook for 5–6 minutes, until light golden, then remove from the heat and drizzle over the lemon juice.

Meanwhile, to toast the almonds, heat a heavy-based, dry frying pan over a medium heat. Add the nuts and cook, stirring, for 5–10 minutes, until they start to turn golden brown and smell fragrant. If you're using pine nuts, only toast them in the pan for a few minutes, taking care not to let them burn. Tip the nuts out of the pan and let them cool a little.

Combine the cooked courgette with the toasted nuts, reheated quinoa, pesto and dried cranberries in a mixing bowl and stir to combine. Transfer the warm salad to a shallow bowl and tuck in.

CHICKEN AND MANGO RAINBOW SALAD

This summery salad is light and refreshing, but don't worry, it won't leave you feeling hungry. **SERVES 2**

30g frozen edamame beans

20g raw cashew nuts

25g leftover cooked red quinoa

1 cucumber, cut into matchsticks

1 carrot, cut into matchsticks

1 mango, peeled and sliced

¼ head of red cabbage, shredded

160g leftover cooked chicken, shredded

20g fresh coriander, chopped

the best stir-fry dressing (page 301)

lemon wedges, to serve

First cook the edamame beans. Bring a small pan of water to a boil. Add the edamame beans and boil for 2–3 minutes to blanch them. Drain and refresh under cold running water to stop them cooking and to keep their bright green colour.

To toast the cashews, heat a heavy-based, dry frying pan over a medium heat. Add the nuts and cook, stirring, for a few minutes, just until they start to turn golden. Tip the nuts out of the pan and set aside to cool a little.

Toss together the cooked edamame beans, quinoa, cucumber, carrot, mango, cabbage and the shredded chicken in a large mixing bowl. Divide the salad between two plates and scatter the coriander and toasted cashews on top. Drizzle with the stir-fry dressing and serve with lemon wedges.

SEARED TUNA SALAD WITH POACHED EGGS

This salad is pure protein goodness! **SERVES 2**

1 carrot, cut into 1cm cubes or thin strips

50g green beans

40g leftover cooked Puy lentils

30g leftover cooked quinoa

25g fresh flat-leaf parsley, chopped

15g sunflower seeds

2 very fresh eggs

drop of vinegar (I use apple cider vinegar)

1 tbsp rapeseed oil

2 x 150g fresh tuna steaks

sea salt and freshly ground black pepper

Steam the carrot and green beans for 5–6 minutes, until soft. Let them cool, then tip into a large mixing bowl with the cooked lentils and quinoa and the parsley and toss to combine. Divide the salad between two serving plates.

Place the sunflower seeds in a dry skillet and set it over a medium heat. Let them sit for the first minute, then start to stir them and let them toast for a further 1–2 minutes, until they have darkened a bit. Tip them out of the pan and set aside.

Next, poach the eggs. The key to perfect poached eggs is to use eggs that are very fresh. Fill a saucepan until the water is about 10cm deep and bring it to a steady simmer, then add a drop of vinegar. Crack each egg into a separate small cup. This is where the fun starts! Create a whirlpool in the saucepan with a slotted spoon and gently slide an egg into the centre, one at a time. Cook for 3 minutes, depending on how runny you like your yolks. Gently lift out the poached eggs with a slotted spoon and set aside to drain on a plate lined with kitchen paper while you cook the tuna.

Heat the oil in a non-stick frying pan over a medium heat. Add the tuna and cook for 1 ½–2 minutes on each side, until it's nicely seared on the outside and still rare in the middle. Allow it to rest for a few minutes.

Cut the tuna into slices and place them on top of the salad. Top with a poached egg, sprinkle over the toasted seeds, season with salt and pepper and serve straight away.

115

118

102

SIDES

Side dishes really complete a meal and can bring even the plainest dishes to life. Yet sometimes they can be a bit of a struggle, especially since they are mostly made up of vegetables. But veg don't have to be boring! There's so much you can do with them to make a knockout dish.

COCONUT CARROT PURÉE

This is so quick to whip up and is a great side dish to accompany plain chicken or fish to add something extra. **SERVES 2**

4 large carrots, sliced

2 tbsp chopped fresh coriander, plus extra to garnish

1 tbsp coconut oil

sea salt and freshly ground black pepper

Steam the carrots for 10–12 minutes, until they are just tender. Drain and place in a food processor with the coriander and coconut oil. Season to taste with salt and pepper and blend until it's a smooth purée. Transfer to a serving bowl and garnish with a little chopped fresh coriander.

HONEY MUSTARD CARROTS

I have a little obsession with a fantastic Irish product, Llewellyn's Irish Balsamic Cider Vinegar, so you'll see it cropping up in recipes throughout the book. It's perfect for adding to sweet and savoury dishes and it can also tart up any simple meal or salad. **SERVES 2**

2 tbsp balsamic cider vinegar or regular balsamic vinegar

1 tbsp rapeseed oil

1 tbsp honey

½ tbsp wholegrain mustard

4 carrots, cut into large batons

Preheat the oven to 190°C.

Whisk together the vinegar, oil, honey and mustard in a small bowl. Place the carrot batons in a separate bowl, drizzle over the vinegar mixture and toss until all the batons are coated. Tip out onto a baking tray and roast for 30 minutes, until golden and a little browned around the edges.

CAULIFLOWER MASH

Coming from a girl who grew up on floury spuds, a cauliflower mash gives your taste buds a healthy challenge! I like to use Herbamare in this mash. It's a blend of sea salt, vegetables, herbs and spices that you can find in health food shops, but if you don't have it, just use some salt and pepper instead. **SERVES 2**

1 head of cauliflower, broken into florets
....

2 tbsp nutritional yeast
....

1 tbsp coconut oil or butter
....

1 tbsp Herbamare seasoning
....

freshly ground black pepper
....

G V P D

DAIRY FREE if you use coconut oil

VEGAN if you use coconut oil

Steam the cauliflower florets until just tender, then pat them dry to absorb any excess water. Blend in a food processor until they're a smooth purée, then add the nutritional yeast, oil or butter and seasoning and pulse again until combined. Transfer to a serving bowl and grind some black pepper on top.

CAULIFLOWER WITH 'CHEESY' WHITE SAUCE

Cheesy cauliflower was a staple side dish with our Sunday roasts at home, but I had to create a lighter version. I'm still trying to get my dad to come around to it though! This dish also works really well with the savoury cashew cheese on page 295 instead of the 'cheesy' white sauce. **SERVES 4**

1 tbsp coconut oil, melted

zest and juice of 1 lemon

1 head of cauliflower, broken into bite-sized florets

sea salt and freshly ground black pepper

'CHEESY' WHITE SAUCE:

1 heaped tbsp coconut oil

2 tbsp buckwheat flour

about 500ml unsweetened almond milk

30g fresh flat-leaf parsley, finely chopped

3 tbsp nutritional yeast

Preheat the oven to 220°C. Line a baking tray with tin foil.

Mix the melted coconut oil with the lemon zest and juice in a small bowl. Place the cauliflower on the lined baking tray, drizzle it with the lemony oil and season with salt and pepper. Roast for 20 minutes, until the cauliflower is golden and tender. Transfer the roasted cauliflower to a serving dish with raised sides.

To make the 'cheesy' white sauce, melt the coconut oil in a saucepan set over a medium heat. Once it has melted add the buckwheat flour and stir to combine, then cook for 1–2 minutes so it loses its raw flour flavour. Slowly pour in the almond milk 125ml at a time, whisking continuously to make sure no lumps form. Keep stirring until it's a thick, creamy consistency. Stir in the chopped parsley and nutritional yeast and season to taste with salt and pepper.

Pour the sauce over the cauliflower and serve straight away.

MEXICAN CAULIFLOWER RICE

Easy to whip up and great for freezing too, cauliflower rice is a game changer. When you mix it with herbs and spices, you could almost trick yourself into thinking you're eating rice! **SERVES 2**

1 head of cauliflower, broken into florets
....

1 tbsp coconut oil
....

½ small red onion, finely chopped
....

1 fresh red chilli, deseeded and finely chopped
....

1 garlic clove, crushed
....

1 ear of fresh corn on the cob
....

100g tinned black beans, drained and rinsed
....

1 tsp ground cumin
....

½ tsp chilli powder
....

8 cherry tomatoes, quartered
....

½ ripe avocado, peeled, stoned and diced
....

25g fresh coriander, roughly chopped
....

juice of ½ lime
....

Place the cauliflower in a food processor and pulse briefly until it looks like rice.

Heat the oil in a large pan over a medium heat. Add the onion and cook for 1–2 minutes, then add the chilli and garlic and cook for 2–3 minutes more.

While that's cooking, cut the corn off the cob using a sharp knife. Add the corn kernels, black beans and spices to the pan along with the riced cauliflower. Cook for just 1 minute – the cauliflower will turn yellow. Remove the pan from the heat and stir in the cherry tomatoes, diced avocado, coriander and lime juice.

PROPER BAKED BEANS

Baked beans made from scratch lack the sugar, salt and additives that are in your favourite tin of beans. Tinned baked beans are convenient and they might seem healthy enough at first glance, but some brands clock up a whopping 13g of sugar per serving. But sure, it's only beans and some tomato. Homemade baked beans are a simple alternative that are more flavoursome than the traditional tinned version and they're a lot more nutritious too. **SERVES 4**

6 large vine-ripened tomatoes, halved
....

500g cherry tomatoes
....

coconut, rapeseed or extra virgin olive oil, for roasting and frying
....

1 small onion, finely chopped
....

2 tsp smoked paprika
....

1 tsp ground cumin
....

½ tsp chilli powder
....

1 tbsp honey or maple syrup
....

1 tbsp Dijon mustard
....

1 tbsp tamari or soya sauce
....

2 x 400g tins of haricot beans, drained and rinsed
....

VEGAN if you use maple syrup

GLUTEN FREE if you use tamari

Preheat the oven to 200°C.

Place the tomatoes on a baking tray, cut side up (leave the cherry tomatoes whole). Drizzle a little oil over them and roast them in the oven for 25 minutes, until the halved tomatoes are golden brown around the edges and the cherry tomatoes have started to burst.

Meanwhile, melt a little coconut oil in a saucepan over a medium heat. Sauté the onion for 10 minutes, until translucent, then stir in the spices and cook for 3–5 minutes more. Stir in the roasted tomatoes, honey, mustard and tamari and cook for a further 3 minutes. Transfer to a powerful blender (I use a NutriBullet) and blend into a smooth sauce.

Put the sauce back in the pan and add the haricot beans. Bring to a boil, then reduce the heat and cook, stirring, for 2–3 minutes.

SWEET POTATO SALAD

I hate having to pass on potato salad. It's such a satisfying, carb-heavy side dish. But the good news is that the alternative actually tastes better than the original. The sweetness of the potatoes and the sharpness of the mustard give it tons of flavour. Put this on the list for your next BBQ! **SERVES 4**

2 sweet potatoes, peeled and cut into 1cm cubes

4 tbsp mayo (homemade on page 300 or shop-bought)

1 tbsp wholegrain mustard

1 tbsp freshly squeezed lemon juice

sea salt

G P D

Bring a saucepan of water to the boil, then tip in the sweet potatoes. Boil hard for 2 minutes, until they're just cooked but aren't breaking up. Drain well and let them cool.

Mix together the mayo, mustard and lemon juice in a large bowl until thoroughly combined. Stir in the sweet potatoes until they're all coated with the dressing, then season with salt.

BROCCOLI AND BEANSPROUTS

Finding it hard to eat your greens? It just takes a few easy steps to turn that around! Start with this recipe. **SERVES 2**

1 tbsp toasted sesame oil

2.5cm piece of fresh root ginger, peeled and grated

1 garlic clove, crushed

200g broccoli florets

150g beansprouts

½ tsp chilli flakes

3 tbsp rice vinegar

2 tbsp tamari

1 tbsp honey or maple syrup

VEGAN if you use maple syrup

Warm the sesame oil in a large frying pan over a high heat. Add the ginger and garlic and cook for 1–2 minutes, until fragrant, then add the broccoli and cook for 1 minute more. Toss in the beansprouts and chilli flakes and cook for a further 2 minutes. Remove from the heat and stir in the rice vinegar, tamari and honey.

SWEET BRAISED CABBAGE

This is a great way to eat cabbage, which is very low in fat and calories. I once lived with a model in Cape Town who made a similar dish, although I'm pretty sure she was sneaking some sugar in there! **SERVES 4**

1 tbsp coconut oil

1 onion, finely chopped

1 cinnamon stick

1 small head of Savoy cabbage, cored and shredded

1 large eating apple, grated

80g raisins

2 tbsp balsamic cider vinegar (or regular balsamic vinegar mixed with 1 tbsp honey or maple syrup)

sea salt and freshly ground black pepper

Melt the coconut oil in a large pan over a low heat. Add the onion and cinnamon stick and sweat for 10 minutes, until the onion is soft. Stir in the cabbage and grated apple and cook for 20 minutes, stirring from time to time, until the cabbage has wilted down. Add the raisins and balsamic cider vinegar and season well. Simmer on a low heat for 15 minutes with the lid on. Serve warm.

CREAMED SPINACH

Sometimes spinach needs a little extra oomph. This 'cheesy' sauce is the perfect helping hand. **SERVES 4**

1 tbsp rapeseed oil

3 garlic cloves, cut in half lengthways

2kg baby spinach

juice of 1 lemon

30ml water

2 tbsp light tahini

2 tbsp nutritional yeast

freshly ground black pepper

Warm the oil in a large frying pan over a low heat. Add the halved garlic cloves and cook, stirring, for 2 minutes, until the garlic is fragrant. Raise the heat to medium, then add the spinach and keep stirring until it begins to wilt. Stir in half of the lemon juice, then remove the pan from the heat.

Mix together the water, tahini, nutritional yeast and the rest of the lemon juice in a small bowl, then drizzle this over the spinach. Season to taste with freshly ground black pepper and serve warm.

ROAST PARSNIP FRIES

I never thought the day would come when I would prefer parsnip fries to potato, but then these fries came along! Not only are they the perfect potato alternative, but because they're naturally quite sweet, you won't be left craving dessert. Bonus! **SERVES 2**

---

2 large parsnips, peeled and cut into chips
....

4 sprigs of fresh thyme, leaves only
....

2 tbsp maple syrup
....

1 tbsp coconut oil, melted
....

1 tsp sea salt
....

Preheat the oven to 200°C. Line a baking tray with tin foil.

Place the parsnips in a large bowl. Mix together the thyme leaves, maple syrup, melted coconut oil and sea salt in a small bowl. Pour this over the parsnips and toss until all the chips are coated. Transfer the chips to the lined baking tray in a single layer and roast for 35 minutes, until tender and golden.

CUCUMBER ROLLS

These rolls are great finger food for a party. **MAKES 16 ROLLS**

2 cucumbers

20g feta cheese

handful of fresh coriander

5 black olives, pitted and diced

6 tbsp hummus (page 284)

3 tbsp chopped sun-dried tomatoes

Slice the cucumbers lengthways into thin ribbons using a mandolin. If you don't have a mandolin, you can slice them by hand using a sharp knife – just try to make them as thin and even as possible. You should aim to get about 16 slices.

Blend the rest of the ingredients in a food processor. Spread the filling evenly over the cucumber ribbons and roll them up. Skewer them with a cocktail stick so they stay rolled up and serve on a platter.

STUFFED PORTOBELLO MUSHROOMS

This is a gorgeous accompaniment to any meal as a side dish or as a starter. Portobello mushrooms are thick and meaty with a nice texture that's the perfect base for a stuffing, sandwiches or even as burger buns. **SERVES 2**

10 sun-dried tomatoes preserved in oil, chopped
....

6 black olives, pitted and chopped
....

1 garlic clove, chopped
....

25g leftover cooked quinoa or black rice (optional)
....

20g fresh flat-leaf parsley, chopped
....

10 fresh basil leaves, chopped
....

1 tbsp rapeseed oil
....

1 tbsp balsamic cider vinegar or apple cider vinegar
....

15g pine nuts
....

2 large Portobello mushrooms, wiped clean
....

....

PALEO if you leave out the quinoa

Preheat the oven to 190°C. Line a baking tray with non-stick baking paper.

Put the sun-dried tomatoes, olives, garlic, cooked quinoa or rice (if using), herbs, oil and vinegar into a food processor and blend together, then stir in the pine nuts.

Spoon the filling into the Portobello mushrooms, place them on the lined tray and roast for 20 minutes, until the mushrooms have softened and the stuffing is warmed through.

COCONUT RICE

Rice is really bland on its own, but a few simple tweaks can transform it into a totally new dish so that you never get bored. This coconut rice goes perfectly with the Whatever You Fancy Curry on page 131. **SERVES 2**

100g basmati or brown rice
....

300ml coconut milk
....

3 tbsp raisins
....

2 tbsp desiccated coconut
....

½ tbsp honey or maple syrup
....

....

VEGAN if you use maple syrup

Place the rice and coconut milk in a saucepan over a medium heat. Bring to a gentle boil, then reduce the heat to very low and cover tightly for 15 minutes, until the rice is cooked through and tender. When the rice is done, remove the pan from the heat. Using a fork, stir in the raisins, desiccated coconut and honey, then cover with the lid again and let it sit for a further 10 minutes. The rice should be fluffy, sticky and sweet.

SPICY SWEET POTATO CUBES

This is one of my boyfriend's favourite side orders from the takeaway. It's packed with spice and sweetness and is a warm, comforting side dish for any meal. **SERVES 2**

1 tbsp cumin seeds

½ tbsp mustard seeds

1 tbsp ground turmeric

1 tbsp smoked paprika

1 tbsp chilli powder

2 large sweet potatoes, peeled and cut into cubes

1 tbsp olive or coconut oil

250ml passata (page 302 or shop-bought)

25g fresh coriander, chopped

Preheat the oven to 190°C.

Heat a heavy-based, dry frying pan over a medium heat. Add the cumin and mustard seeds and toast them for 2–3 minutes, until they begin to crackle. Tip into a pestle and mortar and grind into a fine powder, then mix in the remaining spices.

Place the sweet potatoes in a bowl and pour over the oil, then mix together with your hands. Stir in the spices until the potatoes are evenly coated. Spread the potatoes out on a baking tray and place in the oven for 35 minutes, until the potatoes are tender and lightly browned.

When the potatoes are nearly done, gently heat the passata in a saucepan. Stir in the potatoes and cook for 2 minutes more. Stir in the chopped coriander and transfer to a serving dish.

PESHWARI NAAN

I can never resist Peshwari naan, so I had to create this healthier version. However, I will admit that I still have to get it when I go to my favourite Indian restaurant – it's all about balance. **MAKES 2 LARGE NAAN**

65g tapioca flour

55g ground almonds

250ml coconut milk

3 tbsp desiccated coconut

coconut oil, for frying

2 tbsp raisins

1 tbsp honey or maple syrup

VEGAN if you use maple syrup

Mix together the tapioca flour, ground almonds, coconut milk and 1 tablespoon of desiccated coconut in a large bowl to form a batter.

Melt a little coconut oil in a non-stick pan over a high heat. Pour in half of the batter and lower the heat to medium. Cook for 5–6 minutes, until the naan begins to puff up and is almost cooked. Flip it over and cook for 5 minutes more, until both sides are fully cooked through. Repeat with the remaining batter.

Let the naans cool a little before making an incision and filling the bread with the raisins, honey and the remaining desiccated coconut. Reheat them in a warm oven for 5 minutes before serving. Alternatively, you could simply sprinkle the filling over the naan and roll it up, straight from the pan.

It can be all too easy to get stuck in a rut and just boil up some greens to pair with plain meat or fish for dinner. But there's no need to let taste slip away like that.

MAIN DISHES

Simple steps and techniques like adding spices or how you cook something to let the flavours marry together can turn even a simple meal into a satisfying main dish. And whether you're cooking for one or for a crowd, having some healthy, easy-to-follow main dishes in your repertoire will be a real lifesaver.

TURKEY AND CHICKEN

LOW-CARB TURKEY LASAGNE

Lasagne was one of my favourite childhood meals, but this one is a lot more waistline friendly. It's also one of the most popular recipes on my blog. **SERVES 8**

2 courgettes

sea salt and freshly ground black pepper

coconut or rapeseed oil, for frying

1 large onion, chopped

4 garlic cloves, minced

20g fresh basil leaves, roughly torn

1½ tbsp dried oregano

600ml passata (page 302 or shop-bought)

1kg minced turkey breast

250g Greek yoghurt

75g freshly grated Parmesan

Preheat the oven to 180°C.

Slice the courgettes lengthways as thinly as you can (a mandolin is good for this), sprinkle them with some salt and set aside.

Heat a little oil in a deep saucepan over a medium heat. Sauté the onion and garlic for about 10 minutes, until the onion is soft and slightly browned. Lower the heat, then stir in the basil and oregano and cook for a further 5 minutes. Add the passata and bring to the boil, then reduce the heat and let it simmer for 10 minutes, until thickened slightly. Season with salt and pepper, then blend into a smooth sauce.

In a separate pan, heat a little more oil over a medium heat and add the minced turkey, using a spatula to break the mince into smaller pieces. Cook for 6–8 minutes, until browned. Transfer the cooked turkey mince to the tomato sauce with a slotted spoon and stir to combine. Pour the tomato sauce into a medium-sized rectangular baking dish.

Prepare the cheese sauce by mixing the yoghurt and 50g of the grated Parmesan together in a small bowl.

To assemble the lasagne, put a layer of sliced courgettes on top of the tomato sauce in the base of the dish, then cover this layer with some of the cheese sauce. Keep layering until all the courgettes and all of the cheese sauce have been used up, finishing with a layer of courgettes and a light, even layer of cheese sauce. Sprinkle the remaining 25g of Parmesan on top.

Bake for 30 minutes, until the lasagne is bubbling and the cheese on top is melted and golden brown. Remove from the oven and let the lasagne stand for 10–15 minutes before cutting.

SPICY TURKEY CHILLI

This is one of my favourite fast-fix meals and is a regular go-to when I'm busy. It's another favourite from my blog too. If you don't fancy serving it with spiralised courgette noodles, you could use buckwheat or brown rice noodles instead. Or try serving it in crisp lettuce cups or using it to stuff a baked sweet potato. Whichever way you serve it, this is a simple dish with very little prep that doesn't take ages to cook. It's a lifesaver.

SERVES 2–4

coconut or rapeseed oil, for frying

500g minced turkey breast

1 large onion, chopped

1 fresh red chilli, deseeded and finely chopped

1 fresh green chilli, deseeded and finely chopped

2 garlic cloves, chopped

1 tbsp chilli powder

1 tbsp dried oregano

1 tsp ground cumin

1 tsp ground turmeric

600ml passata (page 302 or shop-bought)

1 bay leaf

1 green courgette

1 yellow courgette

sea salt and freshly ground black pepper

handful of fresh coriander, chopped, to garnish

Heat a little oil in a large saucepan over a medium heat. Cook the minced turkey for 6–8 minutes, until it's just browned, using a spatula to break the mince into smaller pieces. Transfer to a bowl with a slotted spoon, leaving behind any excess fat or water.

Pour any remaining liquid out of the pan and wipe the it clean with a piece of kitchen paper. Add a little fresh oil over a medium heat, then sauté the onion, chillies and garlic for 8 minutes, until softened. Add the browned turkey mince back to the saucepan and cook, stirring, for 5 minutes. Stir in the chilli powder, oregano, cumin and turmeric and cook for a further 2–3 minutes. Add the passata and bay leaf and simmer for 15 minutes more.

Meanwhile, use a spiraliser or julienne peeler to make vegetable noodles from the courgettes. Melt a little oil in a frying pan over a high heat and flash-fry the courgette noodles for 2–3 minutes, just until they've softened. Season to taste with salt and pepper.

To serve, divide the courgette noodles between shallow bowls and spoon the chilli on top. Garnish with the chopped fresh coriander.

SHEPHERD'S PIE WITH SWEET POTATO MASH

Make a big batch of this so that you can have leftovers for lunch throughout the week, or it's perfect for freezing too. If you can't find pre-packed minced turkey breast, just ask your butcher to mince some for you. **SERVES 6**

1 parsnip, cut into small cubes

coconut oil, for frying

1 onion, finely chopped

2 garlic cloves, minced

1.5kg minced turkey breast

3 sprigs of fresh rosemary

1 tbsp ground cumin

1 tbsp smoked paprika

200g frozen petits pois

3 tbsp tamari

1 tbsp tomato purée (opt for one that's 100% tomato)

SWEET POTATO MASH:

800g sweet potatoes, peeled and chopped

2 large carrots, chopped

2 tbsp coconut oil

sea salt and freshly ground black pepper

PALEO if you leave out the petits pois

Preheat the oven to 200°C.

Bring a small saucepan of water to the boil. Add the parsnip cubes, reduce the heat and simmer for about 5 minutes, until they've softened a little but are still holding their shape and don't break easily. Drain and set aside.

Melt a little coconut oil in a large saucepan over a medium heat. Sauté the onion and garlic for 3–4 minutes, until the onion is starting to brown a little. Add the minced turkey and cook, stirring to break the mince into smaller pieces, for about 10 minutes, until the meat is completely browned.

Strip the leaves from the rosemary sprigs and finely chop them, then toss them in with the turkey and onion. Stir in the cumin and paprika and cook for 2 minutes. Add the frozen peas along with the cooked parsnip, tamari and tomato purée. Cook, stirring, for 1 minute, then transfer to a medium-sized baking dish.

While the turkey is cooking, you can prepare the mash. Steam the chopped sweet potatoes and carrots for 12 minutes, until soft. Place in a blender with the coconut oil, sea salt and a little black pepper. Blitz until the mash is smooth and creamy.

Add big dollops of the mash on top of the minced turkey in the baking dish. Spread it out smoothly and evenly with the back of a spoon. Drag the tines of a fork across the top if you want to rough it up to make it extra crispy. Bake for 20 minutes, until the shepherd's pie is bubbling and the mash is golden brown.

KICKIN' CURRY

Boneless, skinless chicken breasts can get boring, so variety is key. There is very little nutritional difference between dark thigh meat and breast meat, so don't be afraid of it. Come to the dark side! **SERVES 3–4**

2 tbsp coconut or olive oil

6 boneless, skinless chicken thighs

1 large onion, sliced into thin rings

3 small garlic cloves, minced

2.5cm piece of fresh root ginger, peeled and grated

1 courgette, diced, or sweet potato, peeled and diced

2 tbsp mustard seeds

2 tbsp ground cumin

1 tbsp ground coriander

1 tbsp ground turmeric

juice of ½ lemon

1½ tbsp tomato purée

500–750ml chicken stock or water

6 dried lime leaves

50g flaked almonds (optional)

steamed brown rice or cooked quinoa, to serve

Peshwari naan (page 118), to serve

chopped fresh coriander, to garnish

Heat 1 tablespoon of the oil in a large pot over a medium heat. Add the chicken (you don't need to cut it up, but can if you want to). Cook for 5–7 minutes, until browned. Transfer to a plate and set aside.

Add the remaining tablespoon of oil and sauté the onion, garlic and ginger for about 10 minutes, stirring, until the onions have softened and turned translucent. Add the diced courgette or sweet potato and all the spices. Stir to combine and cook for 2–3 minutes. Add the lemon juice and tomato purée and mix well before adding just enough chicken stock or water to cover the top of the chicken – you'll probably need 500–750ml, depending on the size of your pot. Lastly, stir in the dried lime leaves.

Bring the curry up to a boil, then reduce the heat to low and let it simmer for about 45 minutes, until the chicken is cooked through and tender. Stir in the flaked almonds at this point if you're using them.

Ladle the curry over a bed of steamed rice or cooked quinoa in a shallow bowl. Serve with Peshwari naan on the side and garnish with some chopped fresh coriander.

KATSU CURRY

Crispy chicken in a creamy sauce is one of those devastatingly delicious meals that I normally associate with people ordering when they're hungover. This no longer has to be a hangover cure, but an everyday blessing! **SERVES 4**

2 eggs

125ml unsweetened almond milk

1 tsp apple cider vinegar

4 chicken fillets

120g buckwheat flour

50g desiccated coconut

pinch of sea salt

CURRY SAUCE:

coconut oil, for frying

2 small fresh green chillies, deseeded and finely chopped

2 garlic cloves, crushed

5 curry leaves

1 tsp ground turmeric

1 tsp coriander seeds or ground coriander

1 tsp cumin seeds

½ tsp curry powder

1 x 400ml tin of full-fat coconut milk

80g cashew butter

spinach, avocado and orange salad with chickpea 'croutons' (page 092) or roast parsnip fries (page 112), to serve

To prepare the chicken, whisk together the eggs, almond milk and vinegar in a large bowl. Pierce each chicken fillet a few times with a fork, then place the chicken in the bowl and let it sit in the egg mix for 30 minutes.

Preheat the oven to 200°C. Line a baking tray with non-stick baking paper.

Put the buckwheat flour, desiccated coconut and a pinch of salt in a ziplock bag and shake to combine. Put the chicken fillets in the bag one at a time and press firmly to make sure they are completely coated in the flour mixture. Place the coated fillets on the lined baking tray. Cook in the oven for 15 minutes, then remove the tray from the oven and turn the fillets over. Put the tray back in the oven and cook for about 10 minutes more, until the chicken is golden and fully cooked.

Meanwhile, to make the curry sauce, melt a little coconut oil in a large saucepan over a low heat. Add the chillies and garlic and cook for 3–5 minutes, until softened. Add the curry leaves and spices and cook for 2 minutes, stirring to toast the seeds and release their flavours. Pour in the coconut milk, reduce the heat and let it simmer for 15 minutes. Remove from the heat and stir in the cashew butter.

Transfer to a blender or use a hand-held blender to blitz the sauce until it's completely smooth. The sauce should be green, so don't worry! Return the sauce to the pan and bring it back up to a gentle simmer. Keep stirring to make sure the sauce doesn't catch on the bottom of the pan and burn, as it should be thick and creamy now.

I like to serve this curry with the spinach, avocado and orange salad on page 92 or poured over roast parsnip fries.

WHATEVER YOU FANCY CURRY

You can use whatever meat or fish you like in this curry: 6 diced chicken fillets; 1kg diced beef (but not stewing beef); 4 x 150g diced monkfish fillets; or 1.5kg prawns, shelled and deveined. **SERVES 4**

7 whole cardamom pods
....

2 tbsp coconut oil
....

1 large onion, chopped
....

1 stalk of fresh lemongrass
....

3 fresh red chillies, deseeded and finely chopped
....

3 large garlic cloves, minced
....

5cm piece of fresh root ginger, peeled and grated
....

10g fresh coriander leaves, roughly chopped
....

1 tbsp ground turmeric
....

1 tsp ground cinnamon
....

1 x 400ml tin of full-fat coconut milk
....

250ml passata (page 302 or shop-bought)
....

your choice of meat or fish (see note above)
....

7 kaffir lime leaves
....

coconut rice (page 116), to serve
....

Put the cardamom pods in a hot, dry, heavy-based frying pan for 1–2 minutes, until they start to crackle. Tip the pods out of the pan and lightly crush them to release the seeds inside, then grind the seeds to a powder in a pestle and mortar.

Melt the coconut oil in a large saucepan over a low heat. Sauté the onion for 8 minutes, until translucent. While that's cooking, remove the outer leaves from the lemongrass stalk and cut away the tough upper half and the base. Cut the stalk in half to reveal the tender core and dice this part. Stir in the diced lemongrass, chillies, garlic, ginger, fresh coriander, turmeric, cinnamon and the ground cardamom. Cook, stirring constantly, for 3–4 minutes. Pour in the coconut milk, reduce the heat to low and simmer for 5 minutes.

Remove the pan from the heat and transfer to a blender or food processor or use a hand-held blender to blitz into a smooth sauce. Return the sauce to the pan over a medium heat and stir in the passata. Add your choice of meat and the kaffir lime leaves. Simmer for 10–15 minutes, until the meat is cooked through. Serve the curry with coconut rice.

PALEO if you don't serve with coconut rice

SPICED CHICKEN LEGS

Chicken legs are really inexpensive, making this a great low-cost meal that's healthy to boot. **SERVES 2**

1 tbsp coriander seeds

4 whole cloves

1 cinnamon stick

1 tbsp paprika

1 tbsp freshly ground black pepper

1 tsp ground turmeric

½ tbsp chilli powder

2 tbsp rapeseed oil

100g natural yoghurt

6 chicken legs or drumsticks or a mix of both

2 bay leaves

garlic 'mayo' (page 300), to serve

Heat a heavy-based, dry frying pan over a high heat. Add the coriander seeds, cloves and cinnamon stick and toast for 2–3 minutes, until the spices are fragrant and start to crackle. Remove the cinnamon stick (but don't throw it away!), then tip the coriander seeds and cloves into a pestle and mortar and crush to a fine powder. Mix with the paprika, freshly ground black pepper, turmeric and chilli powder, then work in the rapeseed oil to form a paste.

Place the natural yoghurt in a large bowl and whisk in the spice paste. Place the chicken legs in the bowl and rub the yoghurt marinade into them, then add the toasted cinnamon stick and the bay leaves. Cover the bowl with cling film and refrigerate overnight if possible – the longer, the better.

The next day, preheat the oven to 200°C.

Tip the chicken legs, marinade and all, onto a baking tray. Cook for 35–40 minutes, until the chicken is fully cooked through. Serve with a dollop of garlic 'mayo'.

CREAMY CHICKEN AND BROCCOLI BAKE

A wholesome, hearty meal that won't leave you feeling sluggish. **SERVES 4**

1 head of broccoli, cut into 2.5cm pieces

1 tbsp rapeseed oil

4 chicken fillets, cut into 2.5cm pieces

CREAMY SAUCE:

1 heaped tbsp coconut oil

3 tbsp buckwheat flour

500ml unsweetened almond milk

sea salt and freshly ground black pepper

3 tbsp nutritional yeast (optional)

TOPPING:

100g gluten-free oats or chopped nuts

2 tbsp milled flaxseeds

2 tbsp melted coconut oil

Preheat the oven to 190°C.

Steam the broccoli for 6 minutes, until it's tender and still bright green.

While the broccoli is steaming, heat a little oil in a frying pan over a medium heat. Add the diced chicken and cook for 8 minutes, until browned around the edges and cooked through. Remove the pan from the heat and set aside.

Now make the creamy white sauce – it's just like making any roux-based sauce. Melt the coconut oil in a small saucepan over a low heat. Add the buckwheat flour and stir until a dry paste forms. Cook for 1 minute so it loses its raw flour flavour. Slowly pour in the almond milk 125ml at a time and whisk continually so no lumps form. This takes patience, but think of it as giving your biceps a little workout. The final result should be a smooth, creamy sauce that has a good pouring consistency and isn't too runny. Season generously with salt and pepper and the nutritional yeast if you're using it for a cheesy flavour.

Place the broccoli, chicken and white sauce in a 20cm x 20cm square or similar size baking dish and mix it all together, making sure the broccoli and chicken are coated with the sauce.

To make the topping, mix the oats or nuts, milled flaxseeds and melted coconut oil together in a small bowl until evenly combined. Sprinkle the topping over the chicken and broccoli and cook in the oven for 10–15 minutes, until the top is lightly toasted all over.

LAMB AND BEEF

SLOW-COOKED LAMB WITH SWEET RED ONIONS, FIGS AND TOMATOES

I'm a huge fan of slow cookers, especially when it comes to cooking lamb. Just turn it on in the morning and forget about it until dinner! This dish gets even better the longer you leave it, so be sure to save some for the next day – it will keep for up to five days in the fridge. **SERVES 4**

2 tbsp rapeseed oil

3 red onions, diced

3 garlic cloves, minced

4 tbsp balsamic cider vinegar or regular balsamic vinegar

3 tbsp honey

2 tbsp tomato purée

1 tsp mixed spice

1 tsp ground cardamom

1kg boneless leg of lamb or lamb shoulder, diced

7 fresh or dried figs (dried figs taste sweeter), halved

5 ripe plum tomatoes, halved

125ml water

3 tbsp chopped fresh thyme leaves

4 bay leaves

2 cinnamon sticks

cooked quinoa, to serve

coconut yoghurt, to garnish

PALEO if you don't serve with quinoa

Heat 1 tablespoon of the oil in a large pan over a low heat. Sweat the red onions for about 8 minutes, until softened. Stir in the garlic, vinegar, honey, tomato purée, mixed spice and ground cardamom and cook for 2 minutes. Transfer everything into a bowl and set aside.

Return the pan to a medium heat and add the remaining tablespoon of oil. Add the lamb and brown it for about 5 minutes. You'll need to do this in batches so that you don't crowd the pan, otherwise the lamb will steam instead of brown. Stir the onion and spice mixture back in along with the figs and tomatoes and cook for 2–3 minutes.

Scrape the contents of the pan into the slow cooker and add the water, thyme, bay leaves and cinnamon sticks. Turn the slow cooker on to a low setting and cook for 9–10 hours, until the lamb is completely tender and falling apart. Serve on a bed of quinoa and garnish with a dollop of coconut yoghurt.

Or if you're pressed for time, here's a speedier way to make this: mix the oil, garlic, honey, tomato purée and spices into a paste and rub it into the lamb. Put the lamb in the slow cooker and pour in the vinegar, figs, tomatoes, water, thyme, bay leaves and cinnamon sticks, stirring to combine. Cook on a low setting for 9–10 hours. The flavour is a little different, but equally as nice.

LAMB MINCE WRAPS WITH MINT YOGHURT

Ireland has some of the best lamb in the world. Did you know that we've even coined a word – lambscape? We should take advantage of what's on our doorstep and embrace this truly organic meat. If you saw me on *Come Dine with Me* back in 2012, you might remember this recipe. It's a healthier take on my best-loved dish from that night, which was a sweet minced lamb stuffed in pitta with homemade relish. **SERVES 4**

25g pine nuts

2 tbsp rapeseed oil

500g minced lamb

1 garlic clove, minced

100g red onion marmalade (page 296)

1 tsp ground cumin

1 tsp ground coriander

handful of fresh flat-leaf parsley, chopped

pomegranate seeds, to garnish

MINT YOGHURT:

200g unsweetened natural yoghurt

15g fresh mint leaves, finely chopped

2 tbsp freshly squeezed lemon juice

CHICKPEA WRAPS:

100g chickpea flour

110ml water

4 tbsp rapeseed oil

2 tbsp tapioca flour

1 tbsp coconut oil

Start by making the chickpea wraps. Place the chickpea flour, water, rapeseed oil and tapioca flour in a medium-sized bowl and mix everything together until you get a thin batter consistency. Melt the coconut oil in a crêpe pan or a non-stick frying pan over a medium heat. Pour in a ladleful of batter and spread it evenly over the base by tilting the pan. Cook for 1–2 minutes on each side, until the edges start to lift up from the base of the pan. Slide the finished wrap onto a plate and repeat with the remaining batter (you should make four wraps). Set aside while you make the filling.

To toast the pine nuts, put a heavy-based, dry pan over a medium heat. Toss in the pine nuts and let them cook for 3–4 minutes, stirring to make sure they toast evenly. Pine nuts can burn quickly, so keep an eye on them. Tip the nuts out of the pan and set aside.

Heat the rapeseed oil in a large frying pan over a high heat. Add the minced lamb and garlic and cook, stirring continuously to break up the mince, for 5 minutes, until browned. Reduce the heat to medium and add the red onion marmalade, cumin and coriander and cook for 2 minutes more. Stir through most of the fresh parsley and the toasted pine nuts.

To make the mint yoghurt, just mix all the ingredients in a bowl until smooth.

To assemble, place a chickpea wrap flat on a plate and spoon about 5 tablespoons of the lamb mince down the middle. Drizzle with the yoghurt and scatter some chopped parsley and pomegranate seeds on top. Roll up the sides or fold the wraps in half like a taco to eat.

LAMB TAGINE

If this looks familiar, it's because you might have seen it as my main course for *The Restaurant* on TV3 in 2015. Lamb tagine is my favourite meal to make at the weekend, when the aromas fill the house. It's the perfect dish for long afternoons when you're taking it easy. **SERVES 4**

1.5kg boneless leg of lamb or lamb shoulder, diced

....

1 tbsp rapeseed oil

....

1 onion, chopped

....

2 garlic cloves, peeled and left whole

....

8 plum tomatoes, chopped

....

1 litre vegetable stock

....

1 sprig of fresh thyme

....

1 butternut squash, peeled and diced

....

50g dried apricots, halved

....

30g fresh coriander, chopped

....

25g fresh flat-leaf parsley, chopped

....

tabbouleh with aubergine, avocado and pomegranate (page 093), to serve

....

MARINADE:

2 tbsp coriander seeds

....

1 tsp cumin seeds

....

2 red onions, peeled and cut into quarters

....

2 garlic cloves, peeled and left whole

....

1 bunch of fresh coriander

....

50ml rapeseed oil

....

1 tbsp smoked paprika

....

1 tsp ground turmeric

....

1 tsp ground ginger

....

1 tsp ground cinnamon

....

....

GLUTEN FREE if you don't serve with tabbouleh

PALEO if you don't serve with tabbouleh

To make the marinade, toast the coriander and cumin seeds in a dry skillet set over a high heat for 2–3 minutes, until they begin to release their fragrance and start to pop.

Put all the marinade ingredients in a food processor, including the toasted seeds, and blitz into a paste. Put the diced lamb in a large bowl, scrape in the paste and stir to coat the lamb in the marinade. Cover the bowl tightly with cling film and marinate for at least 40 minutes or ideally overnight.

Preheat the oven to 150°C.

Heat the oil in a large frying pan over a medium heat. Brown the lamb until it's seared all over, then transfer to an ovenproof casserole. You'll need to do this in batches so that you don't crowd the pan, otherwise the lamb will steam instead of brown. Add the onion, garlic, tomatoes, vegetable stock and the sprig of thyme and cover tightly with the lid. Cook in the oven for 2 hours, then add the diced butternut squash and apricots and cook for 30 minutes more, until the lamb is fork tender. Stir in most of the chopped fresh coriander and parsley.

Ladle the tagine into bowls. Garnish with the remaining fresh chopped coriander and parsley and serve with tabbouleh.

STEAKS WITH BEETROOT AND GINGER RELISH

I don't eat a lot of red meat, but sometimes I just crave a good steak. Steak already has plenty of flavour on its own, but this relish makes a great duo. I usually like to serve steak with cauliflower mash and coconut carrot purée, but you could also try sides like roast parsnip fries (112), garlic 'mayo' (page 300) or red onion marmalade (page 296). **SERVES 2**

2 thick-cut fillet or sirloin steaks

rapeseed oil, for frying

½ red onion, grated

2.5cm piece of fresh root ginger, peeled and grated

1 beetroot, peeled and grated

2 tbsp honey or coconut sugar

1 tsp balsamic cider vinegar or regular balsamic vinegar

sea salt and freshly ground black pepper

cauliflower mash (page 104), to serve

coconut carrot purée (page 102), to serve

Your steak should always be at room temperature before you cook it, so take it out of the fridge at least 30 minutes beforehand.

While your steak is coming back up to room temperature, make the relish. Heat 1 tablespoon of rapeseed oil in a small saucepan over a low heat. Add the onion and ginger and cook for 6 minutes, until the onion is softened but not browned. Add the beetroot, honey and vinegar and season with salt and pepper. Cook for 1–2 minutes more, until the relish has melded together and turned sticky.

Heat a dry, heavy-based chargrill pan or skillet over a high heat. Brush both sides of the steaks with a little rapeseed oil and season generously with salt and pepper. When the pan is good and hot, put in the steaks. Cook a 3.5cm-thick fillet steak for 2 minutes per side for rare, 3 minutes per side for medium-rare and 4 ½ minutes per side for medium. Cook a sirloin steak for 3 minutes per side. Remove from the pan and let the steaks rest for at least 5 minutes so that they stay juicy.

Spoon the relish over the steaks and serve with your choice of sides.

PRE-RACE CHILLI WITH SWEET POTATO CRISPS

This is what I always eat, served with rice, the night before a race or a long cycle.

SERVES 4

coconut or rapeseed oil, for frying
. . . .

1 large onion, chopped
. . . .

1 large fresh red chilli, deseeded and finely chopped
. . . .

2 large garlic cloves, chopped
. . . .

1 tbsp ground cumin
. . . .

1 tbsp sweet or smoked paprika
. . . .

1 tbsp chilli powder
. . . .

1 tsp dried oregano
. . . .

450g minced beef or turkey
. . . .

450ml red pepper passata (page 302)
. . . .

1 tsp hot sauce (optional)
. . . .

200g tinned chickpeas or kidney beans, drained and rinsed
. . . .

cashew cheese with sweet red pepper (page 294), to serve
. . . .

guacamole (page 288), to serve
. . . .

cooked fresh corn on the cob, to serve
. . . .

SWEET POTATO CRISPS:

2 large sweet potatoes, unpeeled
. . . .

2 tbsp rapeseed oil or melted coconut oil
. . . .

1 tbsp dried oregano
. . . .

sea salt and freshly ground black pepper
. . . .

pinch of cayenne pepper (optional)
. . . .

PALEO if you leave out the beans and cashew cheese

Heat a little oil in a large pot over a medium heat. Sauté the onion, chilli, garlic and spices for 5–6 minutes, until the onions are softened and slightly browned. Add the minced meat and stir to break it up. Reduce the heat to low and cook slowly for about 20 minutes, stirring now and then so the meat doesn't catch on the bottom of the pot and burn. Add the passata and hot suace, if using, and bring to the boil for 2 minutes, then reduce the heat and let it simmer for 15 minutes. Add the chickpeas or beans and simmer for another 5 minutes.

While the chilli is simmering, preheat the oven to 200°C to make the sweet potato crisps. Line a baking tray with non-stick baking paper.

Slice the sweet potatoes as thinly as possible with a mandolin or using the slicing blade of your food processor. Place them in a large mixing bowl and toss them in the oil and oregano, then spread them out on the tray, leaving room between each slice to allow them to crisp up in the oven (you might need to use two trays if your trays are small). Season well with salt and pepper and a pinch of cayenne pepper too if you want to give them a little kick. Cook in the oven for 15 minutes, then remove the trays and turn over all the slices. Put the trays back in the oven and cook for 15 minutes more, keeping a close eye on them now to make sure they don't burn. Turn off the heat and leave the trays in the oven for 10 more minutes to let them dry out and crisp up.

To serve, ladle the chilli into bowls and garnish with a dollop of the cashew cheese. Serve with a separate bowl of sweet potato crisps on the side, a bowl of guacamole and some cooked fresh corn on the cob drizzled with a little melted coconut oil and dusted with paprika.

SEAFOOD

ALMOND-CRUSTED BAKED HAKE

White fish needs a bit of a push to get the best flavour from it and to make sure your taste buds are satisfied. This crunchy crust gives hake a great boost, but it would also work just as well with cod. This recipe makes enough for one serving, so just scale it up as needed. **SERVES 1**

40g raw almonds

6 sun-dried tomatoes preserved in olive oil

10g fresh flat-leaf parsley, chopped, plus extra to garnish

zest of 1 lemon

1 tbsp coconut or rapeseed oil

1 tsp chilli flakes (optional)

1 x 120g hake fillet

2 tbsp freshly squeezed lemon juice

sea salt and freshly ground black pepper

lemon wedges, to serve

Preheat the oven to 180°C. Line a baking tray with non-stick baking paper.

Scatter the almonds on a seperate, unlined baking tray in a single layer. Place in the oven for 8–10 minutes to toast them.

Place the sun-dried tomatoes, parsley, lemon zest and oil in a food processor and pulse briefly to blend. Add the almonds and pulse again for 10 seconds – you should now have a chunky paste. Add the chilli flakes, if using, and pulse briefly one more time just to combine.

Place the hake on the lined tray. Drizzle with the lemon juice and season with salt and pepper. Bake for 5 minutes, then remove from the oven, spread the paste evenly over the top of the hake and place it back in the oven for another 7–10 minutes, until it's cooked through. Garnish with a little fresh chopped parsley and serve with a lemon wedge on the side.

SALMON BALLS WITH LEMON AND DILL

If I'm feeling especially organised, I'll make this mix in the morning and leave it in the fridge for later. Even though it's just salmon and a few little extras, these balls have so much flavour that they almost taste meaty. **MAKES 8 BALLS**

2 large skinless, boneless salmon fillets
....

1 garlic clove, peeled
....

handful of fresh dill, chopped, or snipped fresh chives
....

zest and juice of 1 lemon
....

1 tbsp capers (optional)
....

1 tsp Dijon mustard
....

1 tbsp coconut oil
....

grated radishes, to serve
....

homemade mayo (page 300), to serve
....

sweet potato salad (page 108), to serve
....

Preheat the oven to 190°C. Line a baking tray with non-stick baking paper.

Put all the ingredients except the coconut oil into a food processor and pulse briefly until just combined. Place in a bowl and cover with cling film, then put in the fridge for 30 minutes to let the flavours blend together. Divide into eight portions and roll into balls between the palms of your hands.

Heat a little oil in a non-stick frying pan over a medium heat. Place the salmon balls in the pan and cook for 2–3 minutes, gently tossing them around so that they get browned all over. Transfer to the lined baking tray and cook in the oven for about 10 minutes, until the balls are cooked through.

Serve with grated radishes, mayo and sweet potato salad.

SALMON BURGERS

Why don't I get sick of eating so much salmon? Because I change it up! These burgers are super easy and satisfying, and you can even make them ahead of time.

MAKES 4 BURGERS

2 large boneless, skinless salmon fillets
....

15g fresh coriander
....

1 egg white
....

½ garlic clove, minced
....

1 tbsp grated fresh root ginger
....

1 tbsp tamari
....

1 tbsp sesame oil
....

80g black or white sesame seeds, to coat
....

1 tbsp rapeseed oil, for frying
....

avocado and feta dip (page 288), to serve
....

salad leaves, to serve
....

Preheat the oven to 190°C. Line a baking tray with non-stick baking paper.

Place all the ingredients except the sesame seeds and rapeseed oil into a food processor and pulse briefly until just combined. Divide the mixture into four portions and shape into patties. Place on a plate, cover with cling film and let the burgers sit in the fridge for 30 minutes to firm up.

Place the sesame seeds on a shallow plate. Press the salmon burgers into the seeds, one at a time, and pat them gently to coat them all over in the seeds.

Heat the rapeseed oil in a non-stick frying pan over a medium heat. Fry the salmon burgers for 2–3 minutes on each side, until they're nicely browned. Transfer the burgers to the lined tray and bake in the oven for 10 minutes, until cooked all the way through. Serve with avocado and feta dip and salad leaves.

DAIRY FREE if you don't serve with avocado and feta dip

SIMPLE GRILLED PRAWN SKEWERS

When matched with the right spices, prawns can be so flavoursome. I love to serve these with courgette noodles and a simple red pepper sauce for dinner, but some diced avocado and the garlic 'mayo' on page 300 is another option as a light lunch.

MAKES 3 SKEWERS

1 tbsp rapeseed oil, plus extra for frying

1 tsp smoked paprika

1 tsp chilli powder

½ tsp ground cumin

½ tsp ground coriander

sea salt and freshly ground black pepper

12 Dublin Bay prawns, peeled and deveined (ask your fishmonger to do this for you)

squeeze of fresh lemon juice

courgette noodles with simple red pepper sauce (page 303), to serve (optional)

Whisk together the oil, spices and some salt and pepper in a small bowl to create a paste. Get three metal skewers and place four prawns on each one. Using a pastry brush, coat the prawns in the spice paste and let them sit in the fridge for 30 minutes.

Heat a chargrill pan over a medium to high heat. Brush the prawns with a little oil and cook them in the hot pan for 2–3 minutes, turning halfway through, until they turn pink. Remove from the pan and immediately drizzle with a squeeze of lemon juice.

Take the prawns off the skewers and serve them on top of courgette noodles that have been tossed in the simple red pepper sauce, then drizzle a little extra sauce over the top and finish with a grinding of black pepper.

COLOURFUL PRAWN AND VEGETABLE NOODLE SALAD

This colourful dish will awaken your taste buds. Prawns are perfect for a fast meal because they cook so quickly. The trick to making stir-fries is to have all the ingredients prepped and ready to go before you start cooking. **SERVES 2**

25g raw peanuts and/or raw cashews

225g mung bean noodles

1 stalk of fresh lemongrass

1 tbsp toasted sesame oil

60g mangetout

1 red pepper, thinly sliced

½ red onion, thinly sliced

¼ head of broccoli, broken into bite-sized florets

1 small fresh red chilli, deseeded and finely chopped

1 garlic clove, minced

200g prawns, peeled and deveined (ask your fishmonger to do this for you)

juice of ½ lime

25g fresh coriander, chopped

the best stir-fry dressing (page 301)

To toast the nuts, heat a heavy-based, dry frying pan over a medium heat. Add the nuts and cook, stirring, for a few minutes, just until they start to brown. Tip the nuts out of the pan and set aside.

Place the mung bean noodles in a large bowl or pan filled with hot water and let them soak for 5 minutes, until tender, then drain well (or cook the noodles according to the packet instructions).

While the noodles are soaking, remove the outer leaves from the lemongrass stalk and cut away the tough upper half and the base. Cut the stalk in half to reveal the tender core and dice this part.

Heat the sesame oil in a wok or a large frying pan over a medium-high heat. Add the mangetout, red pepper, red onion, broccoli, chilli, garlic and the diced lemongrass and cook for 2–3 minutes, until the vegetables are just starting to soften. Add the prawns, lime juice and toasted nuts and cook for 2–3 minutes more, until the prawns are just cooked through and pink. Stir in the drained mung bean noodles and most of the coriander, then drizzle over the dressing, toss to combine and serve straight away garnished with a few more fresh coriander leaves.

TUNA STEAK WITH BRAZIL NUTS, HONEY AND ORANGE

Put down that tin of tuna – you'll never look back once you start cooking fresh tuna steaks! **SERVES 1**

juice of ½ orange

1 x 150g tuna steak

sea salt and freshly ground black pepper

coconut or rapeseed oil, for frying

20g Brazil nuts, chopped

2.5cm piece of fresh root ginger, peeled and grated

3 tbsp chopped fresh flat-leaf parsley

1 tbsp orange zest

1 tbsp honey

broccoli and beansprouts (page 109), to serve

Drizzle the orange juice over the tuna steak and rub it in, then season with salt and pepper. Heat a little oil in a non-stick frying pan over a medium heat. Add the tuna and cook for 1 ½–2 minutes on each side, until it's nicely seared on the outside and still rare in the middle. Allow it to rest for a few minutes.

While the tuna is resting, toast the Brazil nuts in a hot, dry, heavy-based pan for 2–3 minutes, until they start to turn golden, being careful not to let them burn. Tip the nuts out of the pan and mix them with the grated ginger, parsley, orange zest and honey. Spread over the tuna steak and serve with broccoli and beansprouts on the side.

VEGETARIAN

QUINOA, SWEET POTATO AND KALE BURGERS

Put these on the menu for your next BBQ! Veggie burgers go well with loads of different sides and sauces, just like their meaty counterparts. Try roast parsnip fries (page 112), guacamole (page 288) or avocado and feta dip (page 288), sliced ripe tomatoes and plenty of salad leaves. **MAKES 10 BURGERS**

100g quinoa

280ml water

1 large or 2 small sweet potatoes, peeled and sliced

220g tinned chickpeas, drained and rinsed

4 large sun-dried tomatoes preserved in olive oil

60g feta cheese, crumbled (optional)

40g kale or baby spinach, chopped

15g fresh flat-leaf parsley, chopped

½ tbsp ground cumin

sea salt and freshly ground black pepper

DAIRY FREE if you leave out the feta

Rinse the quinoa under cold running water to get rid of its bitter coating. Place the quinoa in a saucepan and pour in the water. Cover the saucepan and bring to the boil, then reduce the heat and simmer for 15–20 minutes, until the germ has separated from the seed. Tip the cooked quinoa into a colander to drain off any excess water, then set aside and allow to cool (I keep it covered while it's cooling, which helps it to fluff up).

Preheat the oven to 190°C. Line a baking tray with non-stick baking paper.

Boil or steam the sweet potatoes just until they are cooked through and tender. Place in a large bowl and mash until smooth, then stir in the cooked quinoa.

Place the chickpeas and sun-dried tomatoes in a food processor and blend until smooth. Spoon this into the mashed sweet potatoes and stir until evenly combined. Add the remaining ingredients, season with salt and pepper and combine well.

Shape into 10 burgers, place on the tray and bake in the oven for 45 minutes, until firm.

SPICY MEXICAN BLACK BEAN AND BULGUR BURGERS

The bulgur wheat gives these burgers a nutty taste and the black beans give them a soft texture to create a satisfying burger alternative. **MAKES 10 BURGERS**

60g bulgur wheat

coconut or rapeseed oil, for frying

1 red onion, finely chopped

1 fresh red chilli, deseeded and finely chopped

2 large garlic cloves, minced

100g fresh or frozen sweetcorn

1 tsp ground coriander

1 tsp ground turmeric

½ tsp smoked paprika

2 x 400g tins of black beans, drained and rinsed

20g fresh coriander, chopped

juice of ½ lime

sea salt and freshly ground black pepper

simple red pepper sauce (page 303), to serve

quick hummus (page 284), to serve

Preheat the oven to 190°C. Line a baking tray with non-stick baking paper.

Place the bulgur in a heatproof bowl. Boil some water in the kettle and pour in just enough water to cover the bulgur. Stir in a pinch of salt, then cover the bowl with cling film and let it stand for 20 minutes. Drain off any excess water and fluff up the bulgur with a fork.

Meanwhile, heat a little oil in a large frying pan over a low heat. Sweat the onion, chilli and garlic for 8 minutes, until softened. Add the corn and spices and cook for 2–3 minutes more. Remove the pan from the heat and set aside.

Put the black beans into a large bowl and mash until smooth. Stir in the cooked bulgur, fresh coriander and lime juice, then add the onion mixture and some salt and pepper and mix well to combine.

Shape into 10 burgers, place on the lined tray and bake for 50 minutes, until firm. Serve the burgers with simple red pepper sauce and a dollop of hummus.

BEETROOT, BALSAMIC AND BASMATI RICE BURGERS

These burgers get a really lovely crust around the edges. They're a filling meal and the perfect way to use up leftover rice. **MAKES 6 BURGERS**

4 beetroot

coconut or rapeseed oil, for roasting

sea salt and freshly ground black pepper

150g brown basmati rice or 300g leftover cooked rice

360ml water

3 tbsp pumpkin seeds, toasted

juice of ½ lemon

2 sprigs of fresh thyme, leaves only

handful of fresh flat-leaf parsley, chopped

2 tbsp balsamic cider vinegar or regular balsamic vinegar

1 tbsp coriander seeds

Preheat the oven to 200°C.

Tear off a large piece of tin foil and place the beetroot on it. Drizzle with a little oil, season with salt and pepper and loosely wrap them up in the foil, crimping the edges tightly to make sure no steam gets out while they're cooking. Place the wrapped-up beetroot on a baking tray and roast them in the oven for about 45 minutes, until completely tender – a knife inserted into the middle should slide through easily. Open the foil parcel to let the steam out, but step back from it when you do so that you don't get blasted when the hot steam escapes.

Once the beetroot is done, reduce the oven temperature to 190°C and line the baking tray with non-stick baking paper.

While the beetroot is roasting, you can get going on the rice if you're not using leftover cooked rice. Add the rice and water to a saucepan and stir in a pinch of salt. Bring to the boil, then turn the heat all the way down to its lowest setting and cover the pan tightly with a lid. Cook for 10–15 minutes without uncovering the pan, until the rice is tender. Let the rice sit with the lid on until it's ready to be used.

To toast the pumpkin seeds, heat a heavy-based, dry frying pan over a medium heat. Add the seeds and cook, stirring, for a few minutes, just until they start to turn golden. Tip the seeds out of the pan and set aside.

When the beetroot are cool enough to handle, peel and grate them into a large mixing bowl – you want to have about 250g. Stir in the cooked rice, the toasted seeds and all the other ingredients. Season with salt and pepper and combine well using your hands.

Shape into six burgers and place on the lined tray. Cook for 40 minutes, until firm.

STUFFED COURGETTE BOATS

These boats are a great snack, supper or dinner party idea. The stuffing is also delicious on its own, served as a side dish. Don't worry if you don't have all the ingredients listed. This is the kind of recipe where you could use whatever is lurking in your fridge or in the kitchen press – try mushrooms, sweet peppers or chillies, for example. **SERVES 4**

4 medium courgettes

1 small onion, finely chopped

1 red pepper, finely chopped

5 ripe cherry tomatoes, finely chopped

5 tbsp sweetcorn

2 garlic cloves, minced

juice of ½ lime

handful of pine nuts

4 tbsp cottage cheese

handful of fresh basil, chopped

2 tbsp dried oregano

sea salt and freshly ground black pepper

50g freshly grated Parmesan

Preheat the oven to 180°C. Line a baking tray with tin foil.

Cut the courgettes in half lengthways and scoop out the insides using a spoon (don't throw this away!), leaving a hollow boat. Set aside.

Chop up the courgette flesh that you scooped out and place it in a large bowl. Add the onion, red pepper, cherry tomatoes, sweetcorn and garlic, then stir in the lime juice, pine nuts, cottage cheese, basil and oregano and mix it all together. Season to taste with salt and pepper.

Scoop the filling into the courgette boats and place them on the lined baking tray, then sprinkle the grated Parmesan on top. Place in the oven for 10–15 minutes, until they're nearly cooked through. Remove the tray from the oven and preheat the grill to high, then pop them under the grill for another 5 minutes or so, until the cheese is nicely browned.

RAINBOW 'SPAGHETTI'

This 'spaghetti' works really well with the simple red pepper sauce on page 303 or the vegan pesto on page 301. **SERVES 2**

2 red beetroot, peeled

1 green courgette

1 yellow courgette

1 carrot, peeled

¼ butternut squash, peeled

coconut oil, for frying

sea salt

toasted black sesame
seeds, to garnish

fresh basil leaves, to garnish

G V P D

Using a spiraliser or julienne peeler, make vegetable noodles from the beetroot, courgettes, carrot and squash.

Melt a little coconut oil in a large frying pan over a high heat. Quickly fry the veggie noodles for 2–3 minutes, until they have slightly softened. Season with sea salt and garnish with some toasted black sesame seeds and fresh basil leaves. Serve with your choice of sauce.

SWEET POTATO, LENTIL AND QUINOA TART

This dish is perfect if you're having people over, as you can make it the day before. Then all you have to do is pop it into the oven before your friends arrive and serve it with a fresh green salad. **SERVES 8**

CRUST:

200g quinoa

60g pumpkin seeds

pinch of sea salt

3 tbsp coconut oil or butter

3–4 tbsp water

FILLING:

300g Puy lentils

650ml water

2 large sweet potatoes, peeled and cut into cubes

2 tbsp coconut or rapeseed oil

1 red onion, finely chopped

200g baby spinach, chopped

20g fresh flat-leaf parsley, chopped

2 garlic cloves, minced

1 tsp dried thyme

4 tbsp nutritional yeast or grated Parmesan

1 tbsp light tahini

½ tbsp Dijon mustard

TOPPING:

30g gluten-free oats

handful of raw almonds, chopped

1 tbsp rapeseed oil or melted coconut oil

DAIRY FREE if you use nutritional yeast instead of Parmesan and coconut oil instead of butter

VEGAN if you use nutritional yeast instead of Parmesan and coconut oil instead of butter

Preheat the oven to 180°C.

To make the crust, place the quinoa and pumpkin seeds in a food processor and blend into a fine flour. Transfer to a medium-sized bowl, stir in a pinch of salt and rub in the coconut oil or butter with your hands until the mixture looks like breadcrumbs. Pour in the water a little bit at a time and keep working it together with your hands until a dough forms. Press the dough evenly across the base and up the sides of a 20cm tart tin with a removable base (there's no need to line the tin). Bake for 15 minutes, then remove from the oven and let it cool on a wire rack while you make the filling. Keep the oven turned on.

Place the lentils in a sieve and rinse them well. Put the lentils in a saucepan with the water and bring to a boil, then lower the heat and simmer for 25 minutes, until the lentils have absorbed all the water. Stir with a fork.

Meanwhile, steam or boil the sweet potatoes for 8 minutes, until tender.

Heat the oil in a saucepan over a low heat. Sweat the red onion for 8 minutes, until softened. Raise the heat to medium, then add the cooked sweet potatoes, cooked lentils, spinach, parsley, garlic and thyme and cook for 3–5 minutes to let the flavours combine. Stir in the nutritional yeast or Parmesan, tahini and mustard and mix until everything is evenly combined. Spoon the filling into the cooled quinoa crust.

To make the topping, just mix the oats, almonds and oil together in a small bowl and sprinkle it evenly over the top of the tart. Bake the tart for 25 minutes, until the filling has set and the top is lightly golden. Allow the tart to stand for 10–15 minutes before slicing it. This will keep in the fridge for up to three days.

FAKE-AWAY

FISH AND CHIPS

As far as fake-aways go, I would be a fish and chips kind of girl. This totally hits the nail on the head and satisfies my take-away cravings every time. **SERVES 2**

2 eggs

50ml unsweetened almond milk

300g cod, hake or other white fish, skinned, deboned and cut into fish fingers

2 tbsp flaxseeds

2 tbsp pumpkin seeds

1 tbsp sunflower seeds

2 tbsp ground almonds

1 tbsp mixed dried herbs

sea salt and freshly ground black pepper

roast parsnip fries (page 112) with a dash of apple cider vinegar to serve

simple red pepper sauce (page 303), to serve

Crack the eggs into a bowl, pour in the almond milk and whisk them together. Add the fish fingers, making sure they're all coated with the egg mixture, and let them sit in the fridge for 30 minutes.

Preheat the oven to 200°C. Line a baking tray with non-stick baking paper.

Put all the seeds in a blender or food processor and blitz until they resemble fine crumbs. Tip onto a plate or into a shallow, wide-rimmed bowl. Mix with the ground almonds and dried herbs and season with salt and pepper.

Working with one piece at a time, lift the fish fingers out of the eggs, shaking off any excess, and place them in the almond and seed mixture. Roll them around and press them into the mixture to make sure they are evenly coated all over. Place on the lined baking tray and repeat until all the fish fingers are coated.

Cook in the oven for 15–20 minutes, until the fish fingers are golden brown and crispy. Serve with roast parsnip fries with a dash of cider vinegar and a small bowl of red pepper sauce on the side.

BURRITO CABBAGE WRAP

We all know a burrito fanatic. Show them some love and make them this mouth-watering doppelgänger. This recipe makes just one wrap, so if you have a healthy appetite, be sure to scale it up. **SERVES 1**

1 small sweet potato, peeled and sliced
....

sea salt and freshly ground black pepper
....

1 tbsp rapeseed oil
....

100g minced turkey breast
....

1 tsp smoked paprika
....

1 large leaf of Savoy cabbage
....

½ ripe avocado, peeled, stoned and diced
....

3 tbsp Mexican cauliflower rice (see page 106) or leftover cooked quinoa
....

simple red pepper sauce (page 303)
....

black bean dip (page 290)
....

SALSA:

1 large vine-ripened tomato, diced
....

½ red onion, finely chopped
....

juice of ½ lime
....

1 tbsp finely chopped jalapeño pepper
....

1 tbsp chopped fresh coriander
....

1 tbsp apple cider vinegar
....

sea salt and freshly ground black pepper
....

PALEO if you don't use cauliflower rice or black bean dip

First make the salsa by simply combing all the ingredients in a bowl. Set it aside at room temperature to let the flavours develop while you prepare the rest of the burrito.

Boil or steam the sweet potato just until it's cooked through and tender. Mash until smooth and season with salt and pepper.

Heat the oil in a large pan over a medium heat. Add the minced turkey, smoked paprika and some salt and pepper and cook for 8 minutes, stirring to break up the mince, until the mince is fully cooked. Transfer to a bowl with a slotted spoon, leaving behind any excess fat or water.

Spread the cabbage leaf out flat on a board. Spoon 1 tablespoon of sweet potato mash, the cooked turkey mince, the diced avocado and the cauliflower rice or quinoa down the centre of the cabbage leaf. Drizzle over a little red pepper sauce and add a few spoonfuls of black bean dip. You can either pile on the filling and eat it with a fork, or put on a little less filling and roll it up like a burrito by first folding in the sides, then folding in the bottom and rolling it all up tightly towards the open end at the top. Cut the burrito in half on the diagonal to serve.

QUINOA PIZZA

Like most people, I went through a pizza phase but I came out the other side with the help of this just-as-good alternative. The simple red pepper sauce, red pepper passata and the regular passata on pages 302–303 also work well as a pizza sauce.

MAKES 1 X 23CM PIZZA

CRUST:

2 tbsp milled flaxseeds

220g quinoa

½ tbsp honey or maple syrup

pinch of sea salt

SAUCE:

1 roasted red pepper from a jar

1 tbsp tomato purée

1 tbsp dried oregano

TOPPINGS:

baby spinach

cooked, shredded chicken

feta cheese

nutritional yeast

olives

sliced peppers

Serrano ham

DAIRY FREE if you leave out the feta

Place the milled flaxseeds into a small bowl with 6 tablespoons of water and let it sit for 20–30 minutes, until the flax has bulked up and become a paste. This makes a flaxseed 'egg' that works brilliantly to replace eggs in baking.

Preheat the oven to 190°C. Line a 23cm pizza tin with non-stick baking paper.

Place the quinoa in a food processor and blitz until it forms a fine flour. Tip most of the quinoa flour into a bowl and add the honey, the flaxseed 'egg' and a pinch of sea salt. Mix it all together with your hands until it looks like breadcrumbs. Add 1 tablespoon of water at a time and work it in until you get a dough consistency – you'll probably need about 8–10 tablespoons of water in total.

Dust a board and rolling pin with the remaining quinoa flour. Tip the dough onto the floured board and roll it out until it forms a thin base about 23cm in diameter. Transfer the base to the lined pizza tin and bake in the oven for 15–20 minutes, until it has firmed up and turned golden.

While the base is cooking, make the sauce by just blending all the ingredients together in a food processor until smooth.

Spoon the sauce over the cooked pizza base and scatter over your toppings. Pop it back in the oven for another 2–5 minutes, depending on what toppings you've used. Let it sit for about 5 minutes when it comes out of the oven before cutting into slices so the toppings set a little and don't slide off.

CHICKEN SATAY SKEWERS

If a dish has peanut butter in it, I'm in! I used to order satay a lot when I was out for dinner or getting a cheeky take-away. My version of the sauce is much healthier, so you can drizzle lots on. The take-away never gives you enough sauce anyway!

MAKES 4 SKEWERS

1 tbsp toasted sesame oil

1 fresh red chilli, deseeded and finely chopped, plus extra to garnish

1 garlic clove, minced

2.5cm piece of fresh root ginger, peeled and chopped

160g raw peanuts

½ tbsp curry powder

½ x 400ml tin of full-fat coconut milk

1 tbsp tamari

1–2 tbsp maple syrup

pinch of sea salt

2 chicken fillets, cut into strips

Preheat the oven to 220°C.

Heat the toasted sesame oil in a saucepan over a low heat. Add the chilli, garlic and ginger and cook for just 1 minute, until fragrant. Add the peanuts and curry powder and cook for 2–3 minutes before pouring in the coconut milk and tamari and giving it a good stir. Stir in 1 tablespoon of maple syrup and a pinch of sea salt, then taste it to see if you want to add 1 more tablespoon of maple syrup if you'd like it to be a bit sweeter. Pour into a blender or use a hand-held blender and blitz until it's a smooth sauce.

Thread the chicken strips onto four metal skewers and place on a baking tray or in a baking dish. Pour half of the satay sauce over the chicken and cook in the oven for 25 minutes, until golden all over and cooked through.

Meanwhile, put the remaining satay sauce into a small saucepan and gently heat it through. When the skewers come out of the oven, pour the sauce over as a dressing and serve with a little finely chopped chilli scattered on top.

218

197

180

221

198

212

SIMPLE PLEASURES

Simple little things can have a
big impact on your day – they
are life's little luxuries. The treats
in this chapter are perfect for
sharing...or not!

SWEET SNACKS

Using shop-bought dark chocolate for the protein balls on pages 180–184 is a quick and easy option, but if you want to make the balls vegan, gluten free and dairy free, make them using the homemade raw chocolate in the chocolate peanut truffles recipe on page 187 instead.

JAFFA BALLS

You can also make these as brownies! Just press the mixture into a square baking tin lined with non-stick baking paper, freeze for 30 minutes and cut into squares.

MAKES 10 BALLS

200g raw almonds

7 Medjool dates, pitted

zest and juice of 1 small orange (save some strips of zest for decoration)

4 tbsp raw cacao powder

20g dark chocolate, broken into pieces

Blend the almonds, dates, orange zest and juice and the cacao powder together in a food processor. You're looking to form a sticky, dark brown dough with small traces of nuts. Depending on how strong your processor is, this will take 4–10 minutes and you may have to stop a few times to scrape down the sides of the bowl. Patience!

Pinch off portions and roll into balls between the palms of your hands – you should aim to make about 10 balls. Things will get messy, but it's all the more excuse to lick your fingers! But seriously, do keep a clean tea towel beside you, as the mix will stick to your palms. Put the balls on a plate and pop them into the fridge or freezer for a few minutes to let them firm up before you decorate them.

Melt the chocolate in a heatproof bowl set over a pan of gently simmering water (a bain-marie), making sure the water doesn't touch the bottom of the bowl. Stir until smooth. Dip the top of each ball into the melted chocolate and decorate with the strips of orange zest. Place back in the fridge to allow the chocolate topping to set. Keep the balls stored in an airtight container in the fridge for up to six days.

BANOFFEE BALLS

Banoffee is my favourite dessert. If you love it too, then this little snack is the perfect treat. I get all these ingredients at the Asia Market on Drury Street in Dublin, where they're super cheap. Check out your own local Asian market to find healthy ingredients at low prices. **MAKES 10 BALLS**

200g raw almonds

55g banana chips, plus 10 extra to decorate

8 Medjool dates, pitted

1 ½ tbsp light or dark tahini

1 tbsp maple syrup

1 tsp banana essence

20g dark chocolate, broken into pieces

P

Preheat the oven to 190°C.

To toast the almonds, spread them out on a baking tray in a single layer. Bake for 11 minutes, stirring halfway through, until lightly browned.

Blend all the ingredients in a food processor except the dark chocolate. You're looking to form a thick dough with visible pieces of almonds. Pinch off portions and roll into balls between the palms of your hands – you should aim to make about 10 balls. They should stick together easily and they shouldn't be too wet. Put the balls on a plate and pop them into the fridge or freezer for a few minutes to let them firm up before you decorate them.

Melt the chocolate in a heatproof bowl set over a pan of gently simmering water (a bain-marie), making sure the water doesn't touch the bottom of the bowl. Stir until smooth. Dip the top of each ball into the melted chocolate and decorate with a banana chip. Place back in the fridge to allow the chocolate topping to set. Keep the balls stored in an airtight container in the fridge for up to six days.

NOTELLA BALLS

The epic combination of chocolate and hazelnuts is unbeatable.

MAKES 10 BALLS

125g raw almonds

100g raw hazelnuts, plus extra chopped hazelnuts to decorate

3 Medjool dates, pitted

2 tbsp maple syrup

35g dark chocolate, broken into pieces

P

Preheat the oven to 200°C.

Put the almonds on one baking tray and the hazelnuts on a separate tray. Place them in the oven and toast them for about 10 minutes, stirring them halfway through (the hazelnuts may need a few minutes more, until the skins have started to loosen). Remove the hazelnut skins using the roast-and-rub method: tip the warm nuts into a slightly dampened clean kitchen towel, fold up the sides and rub the skins off using the towel. Set the nuts aside to let them cool a little.

Put the toasted nuts, dates and maple syrup in a food processor and blend until a smooth, cookie dough-type texture forms. This can take 4–10 minutes depending on how powerful your processor is. Pinch off portions and roll into balls between the palms of your hands – you should aim to make about 10 balls. Put the balls on a plate and pop them into the fridge or freezer for a few minutes to let them firm up before you decorate them.

Melt the chocolate in a heatproof bowl set over a pan of gently simmering water (a bain-marie), making sure the water doesn't touch the bottom of the bowl. Stir until smooth. Dip the top of each ball into the melted chocolate and decorate with some chopped hazelnuts. Place back in the fridge to allow the chocolate topping to set. Keep the balls stored in an airtight container in the fridge for up to six days.

STRESS-BUSTER BALLS

Lemon balm is one of the most powerful foods you can eat to help relieve stress. I grow my own on my small windowsill. It smells gorgeous and is great for adding to teas and desserts. **MAKES 10 BALLS**

250g raw almonds

13 Medjool dates, pitted

11 fresh lemon balm leaves

3 tbsp lemon zest, plus extra to decorate

2 tbsp cacao nibs

Preheat the oven to 190°C.

To toast the almonds, spread them out on a baking tray in a single layer and bake in the oven for 11 minutes, tossing halfway through, until lightly browned.

Place all the ingredients in a food processor except the cacao nibs. Blend until a smooth, cookie dough-type texture forms. This can take 4–10 minutes depending on how powerful your processor is. Once everything is well blended, stir in the cacao nibs.

Pinch off portions and roll into balls between the palms of your hands – you should aim to make about 10 balls. Grate a little lemon zest over each one to decorate. Store the balls in an airtight container in the fridge for up to six days.

TROPICAL TRUFFLES

Things will get a bit messy and oily when you make these, so have a tea towel handy!
I prefer to make these into tiny truffles, as they are much sweeter and denser than the
others so a little goes a long way.

MAKES 10 SMALL TRUFFLES

150g raw cashews
....

100g desiccated coconut
....

70g dried pineapple
(unsulphured if possible)
....

raw white chocolate (page
205), melted, or coconut oil,
to decorate
....

coconut chips, to decorate
....

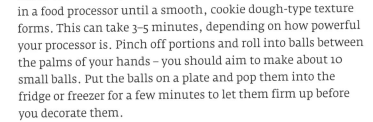

Blend the cashews, desiccated coconut and dried pineapple
in a food processor until a smooth, cookie dough-type texture
forms. This can take 3–5 minutes, depending on how powerful
your processor is. Pinch off portions and roll into balls between
the palms of your hands – you should aim to make about 10
small balls. Put the balls on a plate and pop them into the
fridge or freezer for a few minutes to let them firm up before
you decorate them.

Put a dab of melted raw white chocolate on top of each ball (or
a little coconut oil works fine too) and put a coconut chip on
top to decorate. Store the balls in an airtight container in the
fridge for up to six days.

CHOCOLATE PEANUT TRUFFLES

These truffles were a bit of an accidental discovery, but after the rave reviews I got about them on my blog, I knew they were a keeper. I buy 2kg bags of raw peanuts from the Asia Market on Drury Street in Dublin for €6.50. If you can't find skinless peanuts, just toast them in the oven at 190°C for about 15 minutes, until the skins start to lift off. Then use the roast-and-rub method, just like you'd do for hazelnuts: tip the warm nuts into a slightly dampened clean kitchen towel, fold up the sides and rub the skins off using the towel, then set the nuts aside to let them cool. **MAKES 8 TRUFFLES**

160g raw, skinned peanuts

2 tbsp honey, maple syrup or coconut nectar

2 tbsp melted coconut oil

pinch of sea salt

RAW CHOCOLATE:

140g raw cacao butter, chopped

45g raw cacao powder

4–5 tbsp maple syrup

1 tsp vanilla extract

VEGAN if you use maple syrup

Preheat the oven to 190°C.

Spread the nuts out on a baking tray and toast them in the oven for about 10 minutes, stirring them once halfway through, until golden brown. Set the nuts aside to let them cool a little.

Grind the roasted peanuts in a food processor until they have a fine crumb-like consistency. Add the honey, melted coconut oil and a pinch of sea salt and briefly blend again until mixed well. Pinch off portions and roll into balls between the palms of your hands – you should aim to make about eight balls. Put the balls on a plate and pop them into the fridge or freezer for a few minutes to let them firm up before you decorate them.

To make the raw chocolate, melt the cacao butter in a small saucepan over a low heat. Add the cacao powder, maple syrup and vanilla, remove the pan from the heat and stir until thoroughly combined. Or if you don't want to make your own chocolate, just melt 100g of store-bought dark chocolate (at least 70% cocoa solids) instead, but it won't be vegan, paleo, gluten free or dairy free.

Dip the top of each ball into the melted chocolate. Place them back in the fridge to allow the chocolate topping to set. You won't use all the chocolate, so keep it warm in case you want to add a second coat. Store the balls in an airtight container in the fridge for up to six days.

FAST-FIX PROTEIN BAR

This tastes just like a brownie! These bars won't win any beauty contests, but this quick fix will change your life. It's a handy little recipe for times when you're on your own and want to whip up a small, tasty snack. **MAKES 1 BAR**

2 tbsp raw cacao brown rice protein powder (I use That Protein brand)
....

1 tbsp honey or maple syrup
....

1 tbsp almond butter
....

....

VEGAN if you use maple syrup

Preheat the oven to 180°C. Line a baking tray with non-stick baking paper.

Put all the ingredients in a bowl and mix into a smooth paste. Roll into a ball, then flatten into a rectangular bar and place on the lined tray. Bake for 12 minutes, until browned and a crust forms on the outside. Allow to cool for at least 5 minutes before devouring, as it will continue to harden and set as it cools.

FREEZER BARS

These handy bars are perfect straight from the freezer. **MAKES 10 BARS**

150g raw cashews

125g dried fruit and nut mix

75g raw almonds

80g desiccated coconut

125ml maple syrup

4 tbsp smooth or crunchy peanut butter

3 tbsp coconut water

Put half of the cashews and half of the fruit and nut mix in a food processor and blend until they form small crumbs, like a grainy flour. Tip into a mixing bowl.

Put the remaining cashews and fruit and nut mix in the food processor along with the almonds and briefly pulse for 10–15 seconds, until everything is roughly chopped. Add to the mixing bowl and stir in the desiccated coconut, maple syrup, peanut butter and coconut water. It will be a thick, crunchy dough.

Scrape the dough into a small rectangular tray or plastic container and press down firmly. Cover the tray or container and pop it in the freezer until the dough is hard. Cut into bars when needed and keep them stashed in the freezer. I cut mine after the first hour and then put the bars in a ziplock bag so that I can grab one on the go if I'm rushing out the door – that is, if my sister doesn't get to them all first!

SAVOURY SNACKS

HERBED CRACKER THINS

These are the perfect snack with hummus (pages 284–285) or avocado and feta dip (page 288). They last for two weeks stored in an airtight container at room temperature, so make them in bulk so that you have a steady supply for lunches and snacks.

MAKES 6 CRACKERS

1 tbsp flaxseeds

2 tbsp water

100g ground almonds, plus extra for dusting

2 tbsp mixed seeds

1 tsp dried thyme

1 tsp dried rosemary

1 tsp garlic powder

1 tsp onion powder

Place the flaxseeds in a small bowl with the water and let them soak for 1 hour.

Preheat the oven to 170°C. Line a baking tray with non-stick baking paper.

Put the ground almonds, mixed seeds, dried herbs and spices in a bowl and mix to combine. Stir in the flaxseeds, which should have plumped up into a paste, and combine well to create a dough.

Dust a wooden board with a little ground almonds. Tip the dough out onto the board and divide it into six portions. Working with one portion at a time, roll it out until it's very thin. I like to use a pizza cutter to make the edges of my crackers nice and neat. Repeat with the remaining dough.

Place the crackers on the lined tray, leaving a little space between each one. Bake for 30–35 minutes, until the crackers are crisp and golden. Store in an airtight container for up to two weeks.

GLUTEN-FREE SUN-DRIED TOMATO AND OAT BISCUITS

These biscuits are just the thing to satisfy a craving for something salty. **MAKES 8 BISCUITS**

45g gluten-free oats

4 sun-dried tomatoes in olive oil

1 tbsp sesame or rapeseed oil

1 tsp dried oregano

1 tsp sea salt

2–3 tbsp water

savoury cashew cheese (page 295), to serve

halved red grapes, to serve

Preheat the oven to 170°C. Line a baking tray with non-stick baking paper.

Place the oats in a food processor and blend into a fine flour. Add the sun-dried tomatoes, oil, oregano and salt and blend again until it forms a dry dough. Pour the water through the feeder tube 1 tablespoon at a time and blend again until you get a dough that comes together easily.

Divide the dough into eight portions. Working with one portion at a time, pat it down until it's 0.25cm thick, then stamp out a biscuit using a fluted cutter. Repeat with the remaining dough.

Place the biscuits on the lined tray and bake for 15–20 minutes, until firm, crisp and browned around the edges. Serve with some cashew cheese and halved red grapes. It might sound like an odd combo at first, but it's so tasty. You can thank me later.

CRUNCHY BAKED CHICKPEAS

These are a great snack on their own, but they also make perfect croutons to use in salads. Use whatever combination of herbs and spices you like best. I usually use ground cumin, ground coriander and za'atar, but you could also try smoked paprika, cayenne pepper or chilli powder for a spicy kick or garlic powder and oregano. **MAKES 400G**

1 x 400g tin of chickpeas, drained and rinsed

2 tbsp rapeseed or olive oil

3 tsp mixed herbs and spices (see note above)

Preheat the oven to 200°C. Line a baking tray with non-stick baking paper.

The chickpeas need to be completely dry, so pat them dry with a clean tea towel after you drain and rinse them. Put them in a bowl and coat with the rapeseed oil and spices. Spread the chickpeas out on the lined tray and bake for 40 minutes, until crisp. You can store these at room temperature in a glass jar or airtight container for up to one week.

SWEET AND SALTY POPCORN

If you really want to get adventurous with your popcorn, try adding some cayenne, nutritional yeast and sea salt, or try curry power, cumin and garlic powder. I sometimes use sesame oil instead of coconut to cook the popcorn with, then add a sprinkling of wasabi powder, which I get in my local Asian store. It's so spicy it will clear your sinuses, but it's good! **SERVES 4**

2 tbsp coconut oil

200g popcorn

pinch of pink Himalayan salt or fine sea salt

pinch of powdered stevia

Melt the coconut oil in a heavy-bottomed saucepan on a medium heat, then toss in the popcorn and cover the pan (try to use a pan with a glass lid so that you aren't tempted to peek and let kernels of hot popcorn come flying out!). After 3–5 minutes, once you don't hear the kernels popping anymore, remove the pan from the heat and uncover it. Season the popcorn to taste with the salt and stevia and pour into a big bowl.

TEATIME TREATS

PEANUT BUTTER BANANA COOKIES

These cookies also make a great breakfast on the go. I also love them dipped in some almond milk. **MAKES 14 COOKIES**

2 ripe bananas, peeled

3 tbsp smooth or crunchy peanut butter

2 tbsp coconut oil

4 tbsp coconut sugar

50g roasted peanuts, crushed, or dark chocolate, chopped

200g gluten-free oats

Preheat the oven to 200°C. Line a 32.5cm x 30.5cm tray with non-stick baking paper. That's the size of the baking tray I use and it fits these cookies perfectly, but whatever size tray you have will work just fine too.

Whizz the bananas with a hand-held blender or food processor into a smooth sauce.

Melt the peanut butter and coconut oil together in a medium-sized saucepan over a low heat. Remove from the heat and stir in the creamed bananas, coconut sugar and crushed peanuts or chopped dark chocolate. Mix in the oats until it's like a paste. Pinch off sections of the dough and roll it into balls between the palms of your hands – you should aim to make about 14 cookies. Press down each ball until they're all about 1.25cm thick.

Place the cookies on the lined tray and bake for 13–15 minutes, until golden brown on top and browned and crispy along the edges. Cool on a wire rack for 5 minutes before taking a bite.

TIME-CONSCIOUS COOKIES

In a hurry and need a fast fix? These cookies can be easily whipped up in a blender. You can form these cookies into whatever shape you like. I made them for my friend's hen in some very, er, creative shapes because every hen needs some guilt-free treats! If you make your own raw chocolate, these cookies would be dairy free, gluten free and vegan.

MAKES 12 COOKIES

135g gluten-free oats

70g flaxseeds

1 tsp gluten-free baking powder

10 Medjool dates, pitted

1 banana, peeled

125ml unsweetened rice or almond milk

60g dark chocolate, broken into pieces (or you could make your own raw chocolate – see page 198)

Preheat the oven to 180°C. Line a baking tray with non-stick baking paper.

Place the oats and flaxseeds in a food processor and blend into a fine flour. Tip the flour into a large bowl and stir in the baking powder.

Put the dates, banana and milk into a blender and blitz until a smooth paste forms with little or no trace of the dates. Pour this into the bowl with the oat and flaxseed flour and mix together until a thick, sticky dough forms. Divide the dough into 12 sections and roll each one between the palms of your hands to form a ball. Using your fingertips, flatten into a cookie shape.

Place on the lined tray and bake for 20 minutes, until golden and hard when tapped. Cool the cookies on a wire rack.

While the cookies are cooling, melt the chocolate in a heatproof bowl set over a pan of gently simmering water (a bain-marie), making sure the water doesn't touch the bottom of the bowl. Stir until smooth. Use a spoon to drizzle the cooled cookies with the melted chocolate or dip half of each cookie in the melted chocolate.

TOFFEE POPS

These toffee pops are everyone's favourite. If you make only one recipe from this book, make these bad boys! **MAKES 20 COOKIES**

BISCUIT BASE:

220g ground almonds, plus extra for dusting

3 tbsp coconut oil, at room temperature

1 egg, lightly beaten

3 tbsp honey or maple syrup

1 tsp vanilla essence

pinch of sea salt

CARAMEL:

5 Medjool dates, pitted

2 tsp cashew or almond butter

pinch of sea salt

RAW CHOCOLATE:

140g raw cacao butter, chopped

45g raw cacao powder

4–5 tbsp maple syrup

1 tsp vanilla extract

PALEO if you use almond butter

Preheat the oven to 180°C. Line two baking trays with non-stick baking paper.

Start with the base. Put the ground almonds in a large mixing bowl and rub in the coconut oil with your fingertips until it's like fine crumbs. Add the rest of the base ingredients and mix everything together using your hands. It should be a wet dough.

Sprinkle a wooden board or a clean surface with ground almonds. Tip the dough out onto the board and knead it a few times to bring it together. Pat out the dough until it's 1.25cm thick, then stamp out 20 biscuits with a cookie cutter or the rim of a small glass. Place the cookies on the lined baking trays.

Using your thumb, gently press a well into the centre of each biscuit, being careful not to press the whole way through. Bake in the oven for 20 minutes, until golden on top. The centre dip may rise a little, but don't worry, it will drop again when the cookies cool; if it doesn't, just gently press it back down. Cool on a wire rack for at least 15 minutes.

Meanwhile, put all the caramel ingredients in a food processor and blend until it forms a smooth, chewy caramel ball. Using a teaspoon, fill the wells of the cooled cookies with the caramel, using your finger to gently press it down.

To make the raw chocolate, melt the cacao butter in a small saucepan over a low heat. Add the cacao powder, maple syrup and vanilla, remove the pan from the heat and stir until thoroughly combined.

To finish, dunk the top of each cookie in the raw melted chocolate, place on a plate or tray and put in the freezer for about 15 minutes, until hardened. Store these cookies in an airtight container in the fridge for up to six days.

THE VIRTUOUS VISCOUNT

You could also make these into mint sandwiches – just sandwich the mint filling between two biscuits and dip the entire cookie in melted chocolate. **MAKES 20 COOKIES**

BISCUIT BASE:

220g ground almonds, plus extra for dusting

3 tbsp coconut oil, at room temperature

1 egg, lightly beaten

3 tbsp honey or maple syrup

1 tsp vanilla essence

pinch of sea salt

MINT LAYER:

4 tbsp extra virgin coconut oil or coconut purée

1 tbsp honey

1 tsp spearmint or peppermint extract

RAW CHOCOLATE:

140g raw cacao butter, chopped

45g raw cacao powder

4–5 tbsp maple syrup

1 tsp vanilla extract

Preheat the oven to 180°C. Line two baking trays with non-stick baking paper.

Start with the base. Put the ground almonds in a large mixing bowl and rub in the coconut oil with your fingertips until it's like fine crumbs. Add the rest of the base ingredients and mix everything together using your hands. It should be a wet dough.

Sprinkle a wooden board or a clean surface with ground almonds. Tip the dough out onto the board and knead it a few times to bring it together. Pat out the dough until it's 1.25cm thick, then stamp out 20 biscuits with a cookie cutter or the rim of a small glass. Place the cookies on the lined baking trays.

Using your thumb, gently press a well into the centre of each biscuit, being careful not to press the whole way through. Bake in the oven for 20 minutes, until golden on top. The centre dip may rise a little, but don't worry, it will drop again when the cookies cool; if it doesn't, just gently press it back down. Cool on a wire rack for at least 15 minutes.

Meanwhile, put all the ingredients for the mint layer in a bowl and mix together until it forms a smooth paste. Using a teaspoon, fill the wells of the cooled cookies with the mint paste, using your finger to gently press it down. Sometimes it's easier to roll the mint paste into a little ball and then press it down into the well.

To make the raw chocolate, melt the cacao butter in a small saucepan over a low heat. Add the cacao powder, maple syrup and vanilla, remove the pan from the heat and stir until thoroughly combined.

To finish, dunk the top of each cookie in the raw melted chocolate, place on a plate or tray and put in the fridge until hardened. Store these cookies in an airtight container in the fridge for up to six days.

COOKIE CRUNCH

I always have buckwheat groats in my kitchen press – I adore their crunchy texture. I also call these blackmail cookies because so many of my friends get me to make these for them! **MAKES 16 COOKIES**

450g buckwheat groats

160g desiccated coconut

160g skinned hazelnuts

150g raw almonds

70g cacao nibs

1 tsp sea salt

120g coconut sugar

45g coconut oil

125ml honey or maple syrup

4 tbsp almond butter

VEGAN if you use maple syrup

Preheat the oven to 180°C.

Spread out the buckwheat groats on one baking tray and the desiccated coconut, hazelnuts and almonds on a separate tray. Place in the oven for about 15 minutes, until everything is nicely toasted. Allow to cool.

Reduce the oven to 170°C. Line a baking tray with non-stick baking paper.

Put half of the toasted buckwheat and all of the desiccated coconut, hazelnuts, almonds, cacao nibs and salt in a food processor. Briefly pulse until the ingredients are broken into small pieces but haven't become milled – you want to have plenty of texture, not a fine flour. If you don't have a food processor, you can use almonds and hazelnuts that have been pre-chopped. Tip into a large mixing bowl and stir in the rest of the buckwheat.

Melt the coconut sugar, coconut oil, honey and almond butter in a medium-sized saucepan over a low heat, until the coconut sugar has dissolved and it looks just like caramel. Don't let it boil and don't be tempted to taste it – you will burn your tongue, believe me! Pour into the dry ingredients and mix until everything is well combined.

Spoon a little of the dough into a circular cookie cutter or ring and press it down firmly using the back of the spoon – each cookie should be about 2.5cm thick. Transfer to the lined tray.

Bake in the oven for 15 minutes, until evenly toasted. Let the cookies cool completely before moving them off the baking tray, as this is how they will harden up and keep their shape.

VENUS BARS

You know the whole 'men are from Mars, women are from Venus' thing? Well, these are my take on Mars bars. The last time I made these, I ate six out of the eight bars. Talk about getting high on my own supply! The protein chew layer also works as a protein ball mixed with a few chopped nuts for texture. **MAKES 8 BARS**

THE CHEW LAYER:

2 scoops (60g) vanilla protein powder (I use Ultimate Nutrition, but the Sun Warrior brand is a great option for vegans)

5 tbsp almond butter

2 tbsp honey or maple syrup

CARAMEL:

10 Medjool dates, pitted

3 heaped tbsp cashew butter

2 tbsp coconut water

pinch of sea salt

RAW CHOCOLATE:

140g raw cacao butter, chopped

45g raw cacao powder

4–5 tbsp maple syrup

1 tsp vanilla extract

VEGAN if you use maple syrup

Start with the chew layer. Use a regular breakfast bowl to mix together the protein powder and almond butter with the back of a spoon. Once those are well combined, mix in the honey to make a thick dough. Tip out onto a clean work surface and pat into a 20cm x 10cm rectangle that's 1.5cm thick, then cut widthways into eight bars and set them aside.

Put all the caramel ingredients in a food processor and blend until it's thick, smooth and creamy.

Now comes the fun part: building the bars. Use a teaspoon and knife to spread the caramel over the bars. Don't be stingy here – load it up!

To make the raw chocolate, melt the cacao butter in a small saucepan over a low heat. Add the cacao powder, maple syrup and vanilla, remove the pan from the heat and stir until thoroughly combined. Or if you don't want to make your own chocolate, just melt 200g of store-bought dark chocolate (at least 70% cocoa solids) instead, but it won't be vegan, paleo, gluten free or dairy free.

Line the bottom of a flat baking tray or baking dish with cling film or non-stick baking paper. This is where it gets messy. Using your fingers, dip the bars into the melted chocolate, turning them to ensure they are completely covered. Place the bars on the lined tray, leaving plenty of room between each bar.

Now wait impatiently while it sits in the freezer for 15 minutes, until hardened, before digging in.

OREO BLONDIES

Of all the things I bake, these disappear the fastest – they're a big hit in my house! There are a few different elements to this recipe, but it leads to a seriously satisfying result.

MAKES 14 BLONDIES

WHITE CHOCOLATE CHUNKS:

55g raw cacao butter

45g cashew butter

1 ½ tbsp maple syrup

COOKIE CRUMBLE:

80g skinned hazelnuts

75g raw almonds

2 tbsp raw cacao powder

2 tbsp honey or maple syrup

1 tbsp coconut oil

BLONDIES:

90g gluten-free oats

200g raw cashews

2 ripe bananas, peeled

50ml maple syrup

1 tsp gluten-free baking powder

1 tsp vanilla essence

VEGAN if you use maple syrup

First make the white chocolate chunks. Melt the cacao butter in a small saucepan, then blend with the cashew butter and maple syrup in a food processor until it's a smooth, thick liquid. Pour onto a small tray or into chocolate moulds and place in the freezer for 20–30 minutes, until hard. Chop into chunks and set aside in the fridge.

Preheat the oven to 190°C. Line a 18cm x 18cm square baking tin or two 1lb loaf tins with non-stick baking paper.

Make the cookie crumble next. Put the hazelnuts and almonds in a food processor and blitz until finely ground. Add the cacao powder, honey and coconut oil and blend again until it's well mixed and sticking together. This will take a couple of minutes, depending on how powerful your food processor is. Tip the crumbs onto a baking tray and bake for 8 minutes. Set aside to cool down completely and harden.

To make the blondies, put the oats in a food processor and blend until it forms a very fine flour. Add the cashews and blend again into a fine flour – this could take 4–5 minutes to blend, depending on how powerful your food processor is.

Add the bananas, maple syrup, baking powder and vanilla to the processor and blend until it's a smooth, creamy batter. Stir in the white chocolate chunks and the cookie crumble, then pour into the lined tin.

Bake for 25–30 minutes, depending on how thick the blondies are (using the two loaf tins, mine are about 4cm thick and they take 27 minutes to bake). The blondies are done when the top is set and hard when tapped, with a lovely golden colour. Set aside to cool on a wire rack before lifting them out of the tin, pulling the paper away and cutting into squares. Store in an airtight container at room temperature for up to six days.

ROCKY ROAD

Making homemade marshmallows is surely up there as one of those important life skills that everyone should learn. It can be tricky to get it right, but it will become easier every time you make it. **MAKES 14 SQUARES**

450g dark chocolate (at least 70% cocoa solids)
....

1 x 400ml tin of full-fat coconut milk
....

4 tbsp honey or maple syrup
....

MARSHMALLOW:

250ml water
....

3 tbsp gelatine
....

4 tbsp honey
....

1 tsp vanilla essence
....

BISCUITS:

110g ground almonds
....

1 tbsp tapioca flour
....

30g butter or coconut oil
....

1 tbsp honey or maple syrup
....

You need to make the marshmallow first, so start by lining a 2lb loaf tin with non-stick baking paper. Pour 125ml of the water into a bowl that's big enough to use a hand-held mixer with later and sprinkle over the gelatine, or use the bowl of your stand mixer if you have one. Give it a stir and let it 'bloom'. Pour the remaining 125ml of water into a saucepan with the honey and vanilla. Bring up to a simmer and let it bubble away without stirring for 8–11 minutes, until the colour lightens and the mixture thickens and reduces. Remove from the heat and slowly pour it into the gelatine mix, whisking with a hand-held mixer on a low speed until light and fluffy (this will take 8–10 minutes). Pour into the lined tin and smooth the top until it's level and even. Let the marshmallow sit at room temperature, uncovered, for 2–4 hours, until firm. Lift the marshmallow slab out of the tin, peel away the paper and cut into 2.5cm squares.

Preheat the oven to 180°C. Line a baking tray and a 1lb loaf tin with non-stick baking paper.

Put the ground almonds and tapioca flour into a large bowl and rub in the butter or coconut oil with your fingertips until it forms a crumble texture. Gently melt the honey or maple syrup in a small saucepan or in the microwave and add it to the flour mixture, stirring to combine. Pinch off portions of the dough and mould into biscuits about 2.5cm thick and 5cm in diameter. You should aim to make about eight biscuits. Place the biscuits on the lined baking tray and bake for 10–15 minutes, until golden and firm. Cool on a wire rack, then cut into 2.5cm chunks.

Melt the chocolate in a large heatproof bowl set over a pan of gently simmering water (a bain-marie), making sure the water doesn't touch the bottom of the bowl. Stir until smooth, then remove the bowl from the pan, pour in the coconut milk and honey and stir until thoroughly combined. Mix in the marshmallows and biscuits and stir until they are evenly distributed. Scrape into the lined loaf tin, smoothing the top until it's level and even. Put the tin in the fridge for about 1 hour, until set.

Using the paper, lift the rocky road out of the tin and cut into squares. Store in the fridge in an airtight container for up to one week.

PEANUT BUTTER AND JELLY CUPS

Peanut butter and jelly is another dynamic duo. I always make these for DVD nights in, except I double the batch. It's too hard to stop at just one! **MAKES 8 CUPS**

RAW CHOCOLATE:

280g raw cacao butter, chopped
....
160g maple syrup
....
90g raw cacao powder
....
1 ½ tsp vanilla extract
....

FILLING:

160g skinned peanuts
....
2 tbsp melted coconut oil
....
2 tbsp honey, maple syrup or coconut nectar
....
pinch of sea salt
....
50g raspberry jam (page 304)
....

VEGAN if you use maple syrup or coconut nectar

Preheat the oven to 190°C.

First make the raw chocolate. Melt the cacao butter in a small saucepan over a low heat. Add the maple syrup, cacao powder and vanilla, then remove the pan from the heat and stir until thoroughly combined. Or if you don't want to make your own chocolate, just melt 350g of store-bought dark chocolate (at least 70% cocoa solids) instead, but it won't be vegan, gluten free or dairy free. Spoon half of the melted chocolate into eight cupcake cases (I recommend using a mini silicone cupcake tray) and set in the fridge or freezer until hard.

Meanwhile, spread the nuts out on a baking tray and roast them in the oven for 10–12 minutes, stirring them halfway through, until golden brown. Set the nuts aside to let them cool a little. Grind the roasted peanuts in a food processor until they have a fine crumb-like consistency. Add the melted coconut oil, sweetener and a pinch of salt and briefly blend again until mixed well.

Roll teaspoons of the peanut truffle into balls between the palms of your hands. Press down onto the hardened chocolate in a flat, even layer, making a small well for the jam. Add 1 teaspoon of jam to each cup. Pour over the remaining melted chocolate and put the cups in the fridge again to set and harden. Store in an airtight container in the fridge for up to one week.

BILLIONAIRE'S SHORTBREAD

Donald Trump shared this recipe when I met him while I was modelling in New York... okay, not really. I really did meet him, but we didn't share any kitchen tips. The less glamorous reality is that my aunt always made millionaire's shortbread for me as a child, but I've stepped it up a notch into pure guilt-free gluttony. Just note that if you include the dark chocolate in the filling, it won't be vegan, paleo, gluten free and dairy free.

MAKES 8 SQUARES

BISCUIT BASE:

55g ground almonds

50g coconut flour

3 tbsp melted coconut oil

2 tbsp honey or maple syrup

FILLING:

50g seeds (I use a mix of sunflower, pumpkin and flax)

125g Medjool dates, pitted

125ml unsweetened almond milk

1 tbsp melted coconut oil

1 tsp vanilla essence

pinch of sea salt

35g dark chocolate, chopped (optional)

1 tbsp hazelnut butter

1 tbsp almond butter

1 tbsp cashew butter (or you could use 3 tbsp of just one of these nut butters instead)

RAW CHOCOLATE:

110g raw cacao butter, chopped

30g raw cacao powder

3 tbsp maple syrup

1 tsp vanilla extract

VEGAN if you use maple syrup

PALEO if you don't use cashew butter

First make the base. Line a 1lb loaf tin with non-stick baking paper. Stir together the ground almonds and coconut flour in a mixing bowl, pour in the melted coconut oil and honey and combine well to form a dough. Press into the base of the lined tin and place in the freezer to firm up.

To make the filling, start by toasting the seeds in a heavy-based, dry frying pan set over a medium heat for a few minutes, stirring, just until they start to brown. Tip the seeds out of the pan, give them a rough chop and set aside to let them cool.

Blend the dates in a food processor until smooth, then add the almond milk, melted coconut oil, vanilla and salt and blend again until it's a light, creamy paste. Use a spoon to stir in the remaining filling ingredients, including the toasted seeds. Pour the filling on top of the hardened base, spreading it out evenly and smoothing the top with the back of a spoon. Return the tin to the freezer to firm up the filling layer.

To make the raw chocolate, melt the cacao butter in a small saucepan over a low heat. Add the cacao powder, maple syrup and vanilla, remove the pan from the heat and stir until thoroughly combined. Or if you don't want to make your own chocolate, just melt 80g of store-bought dark chocolate (at least 70% cocoa solids) instead, but it won't be vegan, paleo, gluten free or dairy free. Spread the melted chocolate evenly over the top of the filling and pop the tin back in the freezer again until hard.

Lift the shortbread out of the tin and cut into eight squares. Enjoy with a cuppa and keep the rest stashed in the freezer.

GOOEY CHOCOLATE BROWNIES, THREE WAYS

One brownie recipe, three irresistible variations: white chocolate chunks, berries or caramel popcorn. Decisions, decisions! **MAKES 12–14 BROWNIES**

BASIC BROWNIE RECIPE:

170g ground almonds

....

100g raw cacao powder

....

15 Medjool dates, pitted

....

2 medium bananas, peeled

....

1 tbsp gluten-free baking powder

....

WHITE CHOCOLATE CHUNK BROWNIES:

110g raw cacao butter, chopped

....

90g cashew butter

....

3 tbsp maple syrup

BERRY BROWNIES:

250g blackberries or raspberries

....

CARAMEL POPCORN BROWNIES:

60g popcorn

....

pinch of sea salt

....

25g coconut oil, plus extra for cooking

....

2 tbsp almond butter

....

60g coconut sugar

....

60ml honey or maple syrup

....

G V D

....

VEGAN if you use maple syrup

If you're making the white chocolate chunk brownies, start by melting the cacao butter in a small saucepan, then blending with the cashew butter and maple syrup in a food processor until it's a smooth, thick liquid. Pour onto a small tray or into chocolate moulds and place in the freezer for 20–30 minutes, until hard, then chop into chunks.

Preheat the oven to 180°C. Line a 18cm x 18cm square baking tin or two 1lb loaf tins with non-stick baking paper.

Place all the basic brownie ingredients in a food processor and blend for 5–6 minutes, until smooth. You're looking for a thick batter consistency. You might need to blend it in two batches to make sure it's blended really well.

If you're making the white chocolate chunk brownies or berry brownies, then stir those in now. Spoon the batter into the lined tin. Bake for about 25 minutes, depending on how thick the brownies are (mine are about 4cm thick using two loaf tins). You're looking for them to be set and the top should be slightly hardened. Set aside to cool on a wire rack for at least 10 minutes before lifting the brownies out of the tin, pulling the paper away and cutting into squares. Store in an airtight container in the fridge for up to five days.

If you're making the caramel popcorn brownies, make the popcorn while the brownies cool. Melt a little coconut oil in a heavy-bottomed saucepan on a medium heat, then toss in the popcorn and cover the pan (try to use a pan with a glass lid so that you aren't tempted to peek and let kernels of hot popcorn come flying out!). After 3–5 minutes, once you don't hear the kernels popping anymore, remove the pan from the heat and uncover it. Once the brownies have cooled, scatter the popcorn evenly over the top and sprinkle on a little sea salt.

To make the caramel sauce, melt the coconut oil in a saucepan over a low heat, then add the almond butter and stir until it's runny. Stir in the coconut sugar and honey and raise the heat to medium to bring it up to a gentle simmer. Cook for 2–3 minutes, until the sauce has thickened, like butterscotch sauce. Remove the pan from the heat immediately and let it cool a little before drizzling it all over the popcorn. Place the brownies in the fridge for at least 20 minutes before lifting the brownies out of the tin, pulling the paper away and cutting them into squares.

MINI COCONUT RICE BUNS

I hate wasting food, yet I always overestimate the amount of rice I need. I wanted to come up with ways of putting all those leftovers to good use, and these mini buns are the perfect solution. Plus it couldn't be easier – you just blitz everything in a food processor. If you want to take these up a notch, you can drizzle the buns with a little melted dark chocolate and scatter some coconut chips on top, but using dark chocolate means the buns won't be dairy free, gluten free or vegan. **MAKES 12 BUNS**

300g leftover cooked brown rice

170g honey or maple syrup

2 eggs

1 small banana, peeled

80g raisins

40g desiccated coconut

Preheat the oven to 180°C.

Blend the cooked rice, honey, eggs and banana in a food processor until it forms a smooth batter, then stir in the desiccated coconut. Pour into a mini non-stick bun tray and bake for 20–30 minutes (depending on the size of the tin – small buns will take less time than larger ones). Let them cool in the tray on a wire rack before removing.

CARAMEL BITES

If you're a fan of Rolo candies, these will be right up your street! They knock any naughty cravings on their head, but once you start, it's hard to stop at just one. These are the perfect treat if you're having guests over, to bring to the cinema or even as a gift. They're also a big hit at kids' birthday parties. So think twice about what you would do with your last caramel bite! **MAKES 12**

To make these, you'll need a chocolate mould – I got mine at TK Maxx.

RAW CHOCOLATE:

140g raw cacao butter, chopped

45g raw cacao powder

4–5 tbsp maple syrup

1 tsp vanilla extract

CARAMEL:

200g Medjool dates, pitted

3 tbsp coconut water

pinch of sea salt

To make the raw chocolate, melt the cacao butter in a small saucepan over a low heat. Add the cacao powder, maple syrup and vanilla, remove the pan from the heat and stir until thoroughly combined. Or if you don't want to bother making your own chocolate, you can use 200g of melted dark chocolate (at least 70% cocoa solids) instead, but it won't be vegan, paleo, gluten free or dairy free.

Using a teaspoon, fill your chocolate moulds one-quarter of the way full. You should still have enough chocolate left over to cover the caramel layer later on. Put the mould in the freezer while you make the caramel.

To make the caramel, simply put the dates, coconut water and a pinch of sea salt in a food processor and blend until a smooth, creamy caramel forms.

Once the chocolate layer has hardened up (which should take about 10 minutes), use a teaspoon to spoon a layer of caramel on top. Cover the caramel with a final layer of melted chocolate and put the moulds back in the freezer for another 20–30 minutes, until set. Serve with a nice cuppa.

RAW SUPERFOOD CUPS

This is my absolute favourite 'chocolate' treat and I'm a little protective of it – I've never shared this recipe before now. **MAKES 12 CUPS**

5 tbsp coconut butter

3 tbsp honey or maple syrup

2 tbsp carob flour

2 tbsp lúcuma powder

30g raw macadamia nuts, cut in half

2 tbsp cacao nibs

2 tbsp goji berries

G V P D

VEGAN if you use maple syrup

Melt the coconut butter in a small saucepan over a low heat. Remove the pan from the heat and stir in the honey, carob flour and lúcuma powder. Whisk everything together really well, until it's all thoroughly combined and there is no separation. Stir in the nuts, cacao nibs and goji berries. Spoon into a mini silicone cupcake tray and place in the fridge for about 2 hours, until the cups have hardened. Store these in an airtight container in the fridge for up to 10 days, or you can freeze them for up to two weeks.

Anyone who knows me will know
that this is my favourite chapter
of the entire book. I've always
had a sweet tooth, and growing
up you would rarely see me
without some sort of homemade
cake in my hand or mouth.

DESSERTS

For me, baking is such a creative
process and is the most relaxing
way I could spend an afternoon
by far.

STRAWBERRY AND HAZELNUT CHEESECAKE

My dad makes his famous Australian cheesecake every time I go home. I can't resist it, and once I start, I can't stop. So now we make a deal – I bring the cheesecake, but it's this healthy version. **MAKES 14–16 SLICES**

FILLING:

8 ripe bananas, peeled

750g Greek yoghurt

100g fresh strawberries, hulled, plus extra to serve

1 scoop (30g) strawberry or vanilla whey protein powder

1 tsp vanilla essence or powder

BASE:

350g raw almonds

300g raw hazelnuts

35g cacao nibs

18 Medjool dates, pitted

2 tsp vanilla essence

GLUTEN FREE depending on protein powder used

Preheat the oven to 200°C.

Put the almonds on one baking tray and the hazelnuts on a separate tray. Place them in the oven and toast them for about 10 minutes, stirring them halfway through. The hazelnuts may need a few minutes more, until the skins have started to loosen. Remove the hazelnut skins using the roast-and-rub method: tip the warm nuts into a slightly dampened clean kitchen towel, fold up the sides and rub the skins off using the towel. Set the nuts aside to let them cool.

Reduce the oven temperature to 160°C. Line the base of a 25cm springform tin with non-stick baking paper.

Put all the base ingredients in a food processor and pulse until they are fully combined and have formed a thick dough that sticks together easily. This may take 5–8 minutes depending on how powerful your food processor is. Scrape into the lined tin and press down firmly using the back of a spoon to create an even layer over the bottom (you don't need to press it up the sides of the tin).

Put all the filling ingredients in the food processor and blend until smooth. Pour on top of the base, smoothing the top.

Bake for 45–50 minutes. The top should be set and the cake should be cooked all the way through. Do the wobble test: when you give it a little jiggle, it should be fairly sturdy and firm. A tiny crack will form in the middle when the cheesecake cools, so if you want it picture perfect for your Instagram feed, snap it straight from the oven!

To serve this cheesecake at the perfect temperature, let it cool on a wire rack before chilling it in the fridge for 1 hour. Cut into slices and serve with fresh strawberries.

MANGO, RASPBERRY AND COCONUT CHEESECAKE

The great thing about this cake is that it can be kept in the freezer, so you'll always have a no-fuss dessert ready for when friends call around. **MAKES 8 SLICES**

FILLING:

450g raw cashews

250ml melted coconut oil

180ml maple syrup

zest of ½ lemon

1 tsp vanilla essence

2 mangos, peeled and diced

BASE:

150g raw almonds

80g desiccated coconut

80g buckwheat groats

7 Medjool dates, pitted

1 vanilla pod, split in half lengthways, seeds scraped out and pod discarded

TOPPING:

250g fresh or frozen raspberries

2 tbsp chia seeds

1 tbsp honey or maple syrup

edible flowers, to decorate

VEGAN if you use maple syrup

Put the cashews in a small bowl and cover them with water. Soak for at least 5 hours or overnight.

Line the base of a 25cm springform tin with non-stick baking paper. Put all the base ingredients in a food processor and pulse until they are fully combined and have formed a thick dough that sticks together easily. This may take 5–8 minutes depending on how powerful your food processor is. Scrape into the lined tin and press down firmly using the back of a spoon to create an even layer over the bottom (you don't need to press it up the sides of the tin).

To make the filling, drain and rinse the cashews and pat them dry – you don't want to get any excess water in the filling mixture. Put the cashews in the food processor and blend with the melted coconut oil, maple syrup, lemon zest and vanilla. Add the chopped mango and blend again until it's completely smooth. It will have turned yellow at this point. Pour on top of the base, smoothing the top. Cover tightly with tin foil and place in the freezer overnight (or you can keep it in the freezer for up to one week).

When you're ready to serve, make the topping. Put the raspberries in a small saucepan over a low heat. Once they have started to break down and release their juices, mash them with a fork and stir in the chia seeds and honey. Drizzle over the cheesecake and decorate with edible flowers.

BLACKBERRY CHEESECAKE SLICE

Blackberries give this dessert a really vibrant colour. It's the perfect dessert to make for a party, since it's stored in the freezer and can be prepared days in advance. And yes, in case you haven't noticed, I do have a little blackberry obsession. **MAKES 12 SLICES**

BASE:

200g mix of skinned hazelnuts and almonds
....

200g Medjool dates, pitted
....

70g cacao nibs
....

40g desiccated coconut
....

FILLING:

230g raw cashews
....

125g fresh blackberries, plus extra to serve
....

90g coconut oil
....

125ml maple syrup
....

2 tbsp freshly squeezed lemon juice
....

1 tbsp lemon zest
....

1 tsp vanilla essence
....

Start by putting the cashews in a small bowl and covering them with water. Soak for at least 5 hours or overnight.

To make the bottom, line the bottom of a 20cm springform tin or two 2lb loaf tins with non-stick baking paper. Blend all the base ingredients together in a food processor, then scrape into the lined tin and press down firmly using the back of a spoon to create an even layer over the bottom (you don't need to press it up the sides of the tin).

To make the filling, drain and rinse the cashews and pat them dry – you don't want to get any excess water in the filling mixture. Blend all the filling ingredients together in a food processor until it's a smooth batter. Pour the filling on top of the base, smoothing it out until it's level and even. Freeze for 4 hours, until hard.

Cut into slices and serve with a few fresh blackberries. Keep this stored in the freezer for up to one week.

BAKEWELL SLICE

When I was a child I went through a phase of trying to find the best bakewell tart recipe, so I've had lots of experience making this dessert! In one of my first blog posts, I even did a tour around Dublin to find the best one. Tapioca flour is available in Asian markets, health food stores and the baking section of some supermarkets. It's not 100% necessary for this recipe, but it definitely gives it a better texture. If you can't find it, arrowroot flour will do the job too. **MAKES 14 SLICES**

BASE:

300g ground almonds

3 tbsp butter, vegan butter or coconut oil

1 tbsp honey or maple syrup

1 tbsp tapioca flour

at least 200g raspberry jam (page 304) – the sponge soaks up a bit of the jam, so I recommend really lathering it on

CRUMBLE TOPPING:

50g raw almonds

50g flaked almonds

25g hazelnuts

2 tbsp coconut oil, butter or palm shortening

2 tbsp honey, maple syrup or coconut sugar

SPONGE:

350g ground almonds

1 tbsp gluten-free baking powder

1 tsp ground cinnamon

5 eggs

150g honey

1 tsp almond essence

1 tsp vanilla essence

Greek yoghurt or coconut yoghurt, to serve

DAIRY FREE if you use coconut oil and coconut yoghurt

At least one day before you want to make this bakewell slice, you need to make the jam according to the recipe on page 304.

Preheat the oven to 180°C. Grease the sides of a 18cm x 30cm baking tray with a little coconut oil and line the base with non-stick baking paper.

Put all the base ingredients except the jam in a food processor and mix until a smooth dough forms. Scrape into the lined tray and press it down firmly into a flat, even layer. Bake in the oven for 12 minutes, until lightly golden along the edges. Set aside to cool on a wire rack, then spread the jam over the pastry.

While the pastry is baking, make the crumble topping by pulsing the whole almonds and hazelnuts into a breadcrumb-like texture. Place in a bowl and stir in the flaked almonds. Put the coconut oil and sweetener in a small saucepan and gently heat until the oil has melted, then pour over the dry ingredients and mix together until the nuts and flakes are all coated. Set aside.

To make the sponge, raise the oven temperature to 190°C. Put the ground almonds, baking powder and cinnamon in a large bowl and mix together. In a separate bowl, whisk together the eggs, honey and the almond and vanilla essences. Pour into the dry ingredients and mix together until just combined. Dollop the sponge batter over the jam and spread it out in a smooth, even layer.

Bake in the oven for 20 minutes, then remove from the oven and scatter the crumble topping over the cake. Return to the oven and bake for 20–25 minutes more, until the topping is evenly toasted. Serve with a dollop of yoghurt and a cup of tea.

APPLE UPSIDE DOWN CAKE

This thick cake is really moist in the middle with a crisp edge. Mmm, I'm drooling just thinking about it. **SERVES 8**

1 ½ Bramley apples, peeled

250g ground almonds

4 eggs

4 tbsp honey, plus extra to glaze

1 tbsp gluten-free baking powder

1 tbsp mixed spice

1 tsp ground cinnamon, plus a little extra

1 tsp vanilla essence

coco cream (page 307), to serve

Preheat the oven to 190°C. Line a deep 18cm baking tin with a removable bottom with non-stick baking paper and lightly grease the sides with a little coconut oil.

Grate half of one apple and chop the other half into small cubes. Put the ground almonds, eggs, honey, baking powder, mixed spice, cinnamon and vanilla into a food processor and blend into a smooth batter, then stir in the grated and chopped apples.

Thinly slice the remaining half an apple. Arrange the slices over the bottom of the lined tin in a nice pattern in a single layer (this will be the top of the cake when you turn it upside down). Glaze with a little honey and dust with a pinch of cinnamon. Spread the batter on top of the apple slices, taking care not to move them.

Bake for 50 minutes, until the cake is firm and a skewer inserted into the centre comes out mostly clean – it's okay if a few crumbs are sticking to it. Check the cake towards the end of the cooking time and cover the tin loosely with foil if you think it's getting too browned.

Let the cake cool in the tin on a wire rack for at least 1 hour before inverting it onto a plate and carefully peeling away the baking paper. Serve the cake while it's still slightly warm with a dollop of coco cream.

BALSAMIC, BLACKBERRY AND HAZELNUT CRUMBLE PIE

When I was growing up, we always seemed to have a blackberry crumble in the house during the late summer months because we had a long blackberry hedge the length of a football pitch packed full of berries just waiting to be made into delicious crumbles and jam. Since my birthday is in September, I usually ended up having blackberry crumble instead of a traditional birthday cake, which was perfectly fine with me. I often spent my birthday parties filling baskets of blackberries with my friends so that we could make this dessert. I figured the more hands picking berries, the more crumbles we could have! This recipe has grown up since then, just like me. I've adapted it to give it a healthier spin but without losing any of the fantastic flavour that I remember from those childhood birthdays. **SERVES 8**

BASE:

300g ground almonds

50g desiccated coconut

3 tbsp butter or coconut oil

1 tbsp maple syrup

FILLING:

130g honey or maple syrup

40g tapioca flour

30g coconut sugar

zest of 1 large lemon

4 tbsp chia seeds

3 tbsp balsamic cider vinegar

1 tsp vanilla essence

600g fresh blackberries

CRUMBLE TOPPING:

50g raw hazelnuts

50g raw almonds

50g flaked almonds

50g gluten-free rolled oats or quinoa flakes

20g buckwheat groats (optional)

40g butter or 3 tbsp coconut oil

3 tbsp honey, maple syrup or coconut sugar

Greek yoghurt or coconut yoghurt, to serve

DAIRY FREE if you use oil instead of butter and serve with coconut yoghurt

PALEO if you leave out the oats

VEGAN if you use maple syrup and coconut oil

Preheat the oven to 200°C.

Put the hazelnuts on a baking tray. Place them in the oven and toast them for 10–15 minutes, stirring them halfway through, until the skins have started to loosen. Remove the hazelnut skins using the roast-and-rub method: tip the warm nuts into a slightly dampened clean kitchen towel, fold up the sides and rub the skins off using the towel. Set the nuts aside to let them cool.

Reduce the oven temperature to 180°C.

To make the base, put the ground almonds, desiccated coconut and butter in a food processor and pulse until it forms crumbs. Stir in the maple syrup, which will create a much firmer dough when you press it together with your fingers. Transfer the pastry into a 23cm tart tin with a removable base. Press the dough firmly over the base and all the way up the sides of the tin. Blind bake the base for 12 minutes, until lightly browned. Allow to cool fully on a wire rack.

Put all the filling ingredients except the blackberries in a large bowl and whisk together until it forms a paste. Stir in the blackberries, then spoon the filling into the pastry base, spreading it out evenly.

To make the crumble topping, put the nuts, oats or quinoa flakes and the buckwheat groats, if using, in a bowl and mix together until evenly combined. Melt the butter or coconut oil with the sweetener, then pour over the dry ingredients, stirring to make sure everything is well coated. Scatter the crumble topping over the blackberry filling, making sure it's evenly distributed across the top of the pie.

Bake for 25 minutes, until the topping is golden and toasted. Allow to cool on a wire rack for 10–15 minutes before carefully removing the pie from the tin and cutting into slices. Serve with a dollop of Greek yoghurt or coconut yoghurt.

CHOCOLATE ORANGE TART

The filling in this tart is absolute guilt-free gluttony. If you're not a fan of chocolate orange (I don't get you people!), you can use the raspberry jam on page 304 or the quick blueberry chia jam on page 305 instead. **SERVES 12**

BASE:

220g pecans

150g raw almonds

10 Medjool dates, pitted

3 tbsp orange zest, plus extra to decorate

200g orange saffron marmalade (page 306)

FILLING:

70g raw cacao powder

70g coconut oil

2 ripe avocados, peeled and stoned

3 Medjool dates, pitted

4 tbsp maple syrup

2 tbsp freshly squeezed orange juice

cacao nibs, to decorate

To make the base, put the pecans, almonds, dates and orange zest in a food processor and blend until combined. Press firmly into the base and up the sides of a 23cm tart tin with a removable base (or you could use individual tins). Spread the marmalade over the base in an even layer.

To make the filling, put all the ingredients except the cacao nibs into a food processor and blend until smooth. Make sure no pieces of dates or avocado are visible – this could take 3–4 minutes and you might need to scrape down the sides of the bowl once or twice.

Pour the filling on top of the marmalade and spread it out in an even layer, smoothing the top. Place the tart in the fridge for at least 1 hour to set. Just before serving, scatter over some cacao nibs and orange zest to decorate before cutting into slices.

CHOCOLATE ORANGE MOUSSE

It's actually easier to make this healthy version of mousse than the traditional ones. Get creative with flavours like raspberry, mint or chilli too. **SERVES 4**

juice of 2 oranges

2 ripe avocados, peeled and stoned

2 tbsp honey or maple syrup

1 tbsp raw cacao powder

1 tbsp orange zest

VEGAN if you use maple syrup

Cut the oranges in half and squeeze out the juice, taking care not to break the orange shells and trying to keep them a nice shape. Scrape out any remaining flesh or pith to create four 'bowls'.

Put the orange juice, avocados, honey and cacao powder in a blender and blitz until completely smooth, with no trace of avocado. Spoon the mousse into the hollowed-out oranges and sprinkle over the orange zest. You can keep these refrigerated for up to one day if you want to make them ahead of time. Put the oranges on a pretty plate or baking tray and serve.

SINLESS BANOFFEE

Don't ban the banoffee – try this sinless version of my favourite dessert instead. Although it wasn't the judges' favourite on the night I appeared on TV3's *The Restaurant*, it's still a winner. I like to serve this in old jam jars, small Kilner jars or pretty glasses. Make sure you get a little bit of each layer when you dig your spoon in! **SERVES 6**

BASE LAYER:

250g raw almonds, walnuts or pecans, plus extra to decorate

250g Medjool dates, pitted

2 tbsp cacao nibs (optional)

pinch of sea salt

CARAMEL LAYER:

250g Medjool dates, pitted

125ml coconut water

1 tbsp nut butter

2 tsp vanilla essence

pinch of sea salt

BANANA MOUSSE:

60g light tahini

3 ripe bananas, mashed

2 tbsp coconut oil or butter

2 tbsp coconut water

1 tbsp freshly squeezed lemon juice

2 tsp vanilla essence

coco cream (page 307)

These look impressive, but they couldn't be easier. Start by putting all the base ingredients in a food processor and blending until the mixture is starting to stick together. Spoon into the bottom of the jars and press down with the back of the spoon. Set aside in the fridge while you make the next layer.

Put all the caramel ingredients into the food processor and blend until a smooth, thick caramel forms with no pieces of dates visible. Spoon the caramel on top of the base layer and return to the fridge.

To make the banana mousse – yep, you guessed it – put all the ingredients except the coco cream in the food processor and blend until creamy. Spoon the mousse on top of the caramel as the final layer. (Or you could just slice up some bananas and drizzle them with a squeeze of lemon.) Finish with a dollop of coco cream, scatter over some chopped nuts and serve.

**DAIRY FREE AND
VEGAN** if you use coconut oil

RASPBERRY POSSET WITH PISTACHIO SHORTBREAD

This was the dessert I made when I appeared on *Come Dine with Me* in 2012. Someone asked me for the recipe recently, so of course I had to recreate it as a healthy version. I really experimented with this one. I made a few different versions and this one is by far the best. It emulates the original recipe so well, but without the mountains of sugar and cream I used on the show. This is a great recipe to have up your sleeve for a dinner party, as you can make everything ahead of time before your friends call over. Make extra biscuits – you'll be glad you did after you demolish the first lot! And don't forget to dunk the biscuits into the posset. **SERVES 4**

POSSET:

2 x 400ml tins of full-fat coconut milk
....
250g fresh raspberries
....
juice of 1 lemon
....
4 tbsp honey or maple syrup
....
1 vanilla pod, split in half lengthways, seeds scraped out and pod discarded
....
1 ½ tbsp agar agar flakes (available in health food stores and larger supermarkets)
....

SHORTBREAD:

100g ground almonds, plus extra for dusting
....
30g butter, vegan butter or palm shortening
....
25g shelled pistachios
....
2 tbsp maple syrup
....
1 tbsp tapioca flour or starch
....
½ tsp gluten-free baking powder
....
½ vanilla pod, split in half lengthways, seeds scraped out and pod discarded, or ½ tsp vanilla essence
....

DAIRY FREE if you use vegan butter or palm shortening

VEGAN if you use maple syrup and vegan butter or palm shortening

To make the posset, you need to pop the tins of coconut milk in the fridge for at least 30 minutes so that the cream separates from the rest of the milk. Open the tins just a little and strain out the liquid, leaving only the thick cream (you can use the thin milk for smoothies). Scoop this cream out of the tins and set aside in a bowl. It should be the consistency of thick cream, with no lumps (if there are lumps, just whisk the cream until it's smooth).

While the coconut milk is chilling, put the raspberries in a small saucepan and mash them with a fork. Set the pan over a medium heat, stir in the lemon juice and simmer the berries for 3–4 minutes, stirring often, until the raspberries have completely broken down. Pour the purée through a fine-mesh sieve or muslin cloth – you should have at least 250ml of a thick liquid.

Pour the liquid back into the saucepan and stir in the sweetener and vanilla, then add the agar agar. Bring to the boil, then reduce the heat and simmer for 5–7 minutes, until the agar agar has dissolved and the juice has thickened slightly. Remove the pan from the heat and let it cool for 2–3 minutes before whisking in the coconut cream – if you put the coconut cream in when it's still too hot, it will separate. Pour the posset into glass jars or moulds immediately. Refrigerate for 2–3 hours, until set.

Meanwhile, preheat the oven to 180°C. Line a baking tray with non-stick baking paper.

Put all the shortbread ingredients in a food processor or high-speed blender and blend for about 30 seconds, until a smooth dough forms. You can either form the dough into a ball, wrap it in cling film and put it in the fridge for 30 minutes to make cutting out the shortbread easier, or you can work with the dough straight away if you're shaping the shortbread by hand. Either way, lightly dust a work surface with ground almonds and roll out sections of the dough until it's 1.5cm thick.

Using a knife or a pizza cutter, cut the dough into 8cm x 3cm rectangles. You should get eight biscuits. Place the biscuits on the lined tray and bake for 13 minutes, until light golden. Leave the shortbread on the tray and let it cool on a wire rack for at least 10 minutes to let the biscuits firm up, otherwise they may break.

Serve each jar of posset with two shortbread biscuits alongside.

PROBIOTIC BERRY ICE POPS

Shh, don't tell the ice cream man! **MAKES 4 ICE POPS**

250g natural probiotic
yoghurt

2 tbsp honey or maple
syrup

1 tbsp freshly squeezed
lemon juice

2 handfuls of fresh
strawberries, hulled and
chopped, or other chopped
fresh berries

Mix the yoghurt, honey and lemon juice in a large Pyrex jug. Divide the chopped fruit between four ice pop moulds, then top up with the yoghurt and insert an ice pop stick. Place in the freezer for 3 hours, until frozen solid.

To remove the frozen ice pops from their moulds, fill a deep bowl with hot tap water and quickly dip the moulds in the water to help loosen them.

HONEYDEW SORBET

This sorbet is a wonderfully refreshing, light dessert. I once had a spoon fight over it. Things got a little out of hand. **SERVES 2**

---

1 honeydew melon
....

zest and juice of 1 lime
....

3 tbsp honey or maple syrup
....

VEGAN if you use maple syrup

Cut the melon in half and scoop out the seeds. Cut the flesh away from the hard rind and cut into chunks, discarding the rinds. Put the chopped melon in the freezer for 4–5 hours, until frozen.

Transfer the frozen melon to a food processor along with the lime zest and juice and the honey. Blend until smooth and serve immediately, or pour into a plastic tub with a lid and freeze for up to three days.

PISTACHIO, COCONUT AND CACAO ICE CREAM

If you can't find pistachio butter in the shops, you can make your own by blending 100g roasted pistachios until smooth. This ice cream also works well with almond or hazelnut butter too. For an extra treat and if you're not worried about it being vegan, paleo, gluten free or dairy free, drizzle the ice cream with some melted dark chocolate. **SERVES 6**

50g shelled pistachios, roughly chopped, plus extra crushed nuts to decorate

1 large, ripe avocado, peeled and stoned

1 x 400ml tin of full-fat coconut milk

4 tbsp pistachio, almond or hazelnut butter

4 tbsp honey or maple syrup

1 vanilla pod, split in half lengthways, seeds scraped out and pod discarded

70g cacao nibs

To toast the pistachios, heat a heavy-based, dry frying pan over a medium heat. Add the nuts and cook, stirring, for a few minutes, just until they start to brown. Tip the nuts out of the pan and set aside to let them cool.

Mix the avocado, coconut milk, pistachio butter, honey and vanilla seeds in a blender until completely smooth and creamy. Stir in the toasted pistachios and cacao nibs. Pour into a plastic container that has a lid and place in the freezer for at least 5–6 hours, taking it out and vigorously stirring with a fork every 45 minutes to 1 hour. Serve with crushed pistachios.

VEGAN if you use maple syrup

PECAN PRALINE ICE CREAM

Sweet, crunchy pecans covered in creamy, smooth ice cream – the perfect summer treat. **SERVES 2**

15g raw pecans
....

1 tbsp honey or maple syrup
....

pinch of sea salt
....

3 bananas, peeled, sliced and frozen
....

3 Medjool dates, pitted
....

20ml unsweetened almond milk
....

VEGAN if you use maple syrup

Preheat the oven to 190°C.

Put the pecans in a small bowl and coat them with the honey and sea salt. Spread them out on a baking tray and toast them in the oven for 10 minutes. Let the nuts cool, then break them into pieces.

Put the frozen bananas, dates and almond milk into a powerful, high-speed food processor and blend until smooth and creamy. Stir in the pecans and serve immediately, or pour into a plastic tub with a lid and freeze for up to two days.

257

267

262

BREAD

Ah, bread. It's the first thing everyone tells you to stop eating if you want to have a healthy lifestyle, but that's easier said than done, isn't it? It's practically been bred into us (bad pun, I know!) – tea and toast is a much-loved staple of the Irish diet. But don't worry! You don't need to quit bread altogether, you just need to start making your own. After you get the hang of it, it will be easier to knock out a quick loaf, scones or muffins than to pop down to the shops for them.

SUN-DRIED TOMATO, BASIL AND FETA SPELT BREAD

I use a mix of flax, sunflower and pumpkin seeds in this bread. You can mill seeds yourself in a food processor or coffee grinder or you can buy them already milled. This bread is great with some coconut oil spread on top or mashed avocado. **MAKES 1 LOAF**

230g wholemeal spelt flour

160g milled seeds (see note above)

3 tbsp psyllium husks

1 tbsp gluten-free baking powder

2 eggs

175ml unsweetened almond milk

3 tbsp melted coconut oil

2 tbsp apple cider vinegar

60g feta cheese, chopped

60g sun-dried tomatoes preserved in olive oil, chopped

handful of fresh basil leaves, chopped

whole seeds, to garnish

Preheat the oven to 180°C. Line a 2lb loaf tin with non-stick baking paper.

Mix together the spelt flour, milled seeds, psyllium husk and baking powder in a large bowl. Whisk together the eggs, almond milk, melted coconut oil and vinegar in a separate bowl, then pour this into the dry ingredients and stir until everything is fully combined. It should be a thick dough. Mix in the feta, sun-dried tomatoes and basil – you don't have to be too delicate with this!

Scrape the dough into the lined loaf tin. Smooth the top with the back of a spoon and sprinkle some seeds on top. Bake in the oven for 35 minutes, until toasted on top and firm. Allow to cool on a wire rack before slicing, then store in an airtight container for up to five days.

OAT LOAF OR SCONES

Because we've all grown up with oats we have a tendency to take them for granted, but they are so versatile and can be a wonderful flour substitute. Use this recipe as a base to play with – I've listed a few ideas to get you started. **MAKES 1 LOAF OR 8 SCONES**

180g gluten-free oats

160g milled seeds (I use a mix of flax, sunflower and pumpkin seeds)

1 ½ tbsp psyllium husks

1 tbsp gluten-free baking powder

3 eggs

175ml unsweetened almond milk

3 tbsp melted coconut oil

2 tbsp apple cider vinegar

VARIATIONS:

40g crumbled feta cheese, 30g cooked butternut squash, chopped fresh chives

40g crumbled goat's cheese, 30g whole seeds, 3 tbsp pesto

1 small grated courgette, 30g grated Parmesan cheese, fresh thyme leaves

1 small mashed banana, 20g chopped nuts, 1 tbsp honey

Preheat the oven to 180°C. Line a 2lb loaf tin (if you're making a loaf of bread) or a baking tray (if you're making scones) with non-stick baking paper.

Place the oats in a food processor and blend into a fine flour, then tip into a large bowl. Add the milled seeds, psyllium husks and baking powder to the oat flour and stir to combine. (If you can't find milled seeds, you can do it yourself in the food processor – just blend them at the same time as the oats.)

In a separate bowl, whisk together the eggs, almond milk, melted coconut oil and cider vinegar. Pour this into the bowl with the dry ingredients and mix together with a wooden spoon to form a dough. At this point, you can either leave this plain or use your hands to mix in your add-ins.

If you're making a loaf of bread, scrape the dough into the lined loaf tin and smooth the top with the back of a spoon. Bake for 35 minutes, until lightly golden and a hard crust has formed on top.

If you're making scones, sprinkle a little oat flour on a wooden chopping board. Tip the dough out onto the board and pat it down until it's about 5cm thick. Use a fluted cutter or the rim of a glass to cut out the scones and place them on the lined baking tray. Bake for 25 minutes, until firm and light golden.

G

SESAME BAGELS

These bagels aren't like any bagels you've had before! I love them on their own, but I also serve them with scrambled eggs and they make the best BLTs. **MAKES 10 BAGELS**

coconut oil, for greasing

220g ground almonds

60g arrowroot flour

8 tbsp psyllium husks

1 tbsp gluten-free baking powder

4 egg whites

2 eggs

2 tbsp apple cider vinegar

350ml boiling water

3 tbsp chia seeds

4 tbsp sesame seeds

Preheat the oven to 180°C. Grease a donut or bagel tin with a little coconut oil.

Mix together the ground almonds, arrowroot flour, psyllium husks and baking powder in a large mixing bowl. In a separate bowl, whisk together the egg whites, whole eggs and apple cider vinegar.

Add the egg mix to the dry ingredients. Mix it all together with a fork, making sure there are no lumps. Pour in the boiling water and work quickly to avoid any lumps, once again using the fork to give it a good whisk until everything is thoroughly combined. Stir in the chia seeds and let it sit for 2–3 minutes so the seeds get absorbed into the mix.

Spoon into the bagel tin, overfilling the moulds a little. This is a thick mixture, so don't worry, it won't run off the sides.

Sprinkle the sesame seeds on top of the bagels and press them down a little with your fingertips. Bake for 55 minutes, until firm, golden and nicely toasted.

LEMON AND POPPY SEED SPELT LOAF

There always seemed to be a lemon and poppy seed loaf around when I was growing up. My granny's friend, Anna, used to make the most amazing one. You know how certain foods or meals stay with you forever? Well, Anna's loaf is like that for me. I spent years trying to create this healthy version and I've finally nailed it. **MAKES 1 LOAF**

175g white spelt flour

35g poppy seeds

1 tbsp baking powder

1 tsp baking soda

zest of 2 small lemons

juice of 1 lemon

150ml honey

3 eggs

3 tbsp coconut oil, melted

1 tsp vanilla extract

LEMON GLAZE:

3 tbsp coconut oil, melted

3 tbsp freshly squeezed lemon juice

2 tbsp powdered stevia

2.5cm-thick lemon slices cut into quarters, to decorate

Preheat the oven to 180°C. Line a 1lb loaf tin with non-stick baking paper.

Combine the spelt flour, poppy seeds, baking powder and baking soda in a large bowl. In a separate bowl, whisk together the lemon zest and juice, honey, eggs, melted coconut oil and vanilla. Pour the wet ingredients into the bowl with the dry ingredients and mix everything together until it's fully combined.

Scrape the dough into the lined loaf tin and smooth the top with the back of a spoon. Bake for about 1 hour, until firm and lightly golden. Turn the loaf out of the tin and let it cool completely on a wire rack before drizzling over the glaze (otherwise it will just melt and run right off).

To make the glaze, simply mix all the ingredients together in a small bowl and drizzle it over the cooled loaf. Decorate with the sliced lemon quarters in a line down the middle. Store in an airtight container for up to six days.

BANANA BREAD

I can't even talk about this bread without salivating. We all have a banana bread recipe we turn to time and time again, but I challenge you to try this one and not come back for more! **MAKES 1 LOAF**

2 eggs, separated

5 bananas, peeled

120g buckwheat flour

115g wholemeal spelt flour

60g coconut sugar

12 Medjool dates, pitted

125ml dairy-free milk (I use coconut)

1 tsp vanilla essence

a little honey, to glaze

Preheat the oven to 190°C. Grease a 2lb loaf tin or line it with non-stick baking paper.

In a spotlessly clean, dry bowl, whisk the egg whites until they form stiff peaks. (Using whipped egg whites means you don't have to use baking powder in this bread.)

Put four of the bananas into a blender along with the egg yolks, flours, coconut sugar, dates, dairy-free milk and vanilla. Blitz until completely smooth. You don't want any little bits in the batter, especially from the dates. Pour the batter into a bowl and gently fold in the egg whites, trying to keep as much volume as possible.

Scrape the batter into the prepared tin. Slice the remaining banana in half lengthways, place it on top and glaze with a little honey. Bake for 40 minutes, until the bread has risen and is firm to the touch.

Allow the bread to cool on a wire rack. Wait until it has cooled a little before removing it from the tin, but don't worry, it shouldn't fall apart – it's a very sturdy bread. Wrap in tin foil and keep in the refrigerator for up to six days.

RACHEL'S RAISIN AND WALNUT BREAD

My sister Rachel also loves food and we're the perfect pair in the kitchen – I love to bake and, well, she loves to clean. It's a win-win! **MAKES 1 LOAF**

100g raw walnut halves, plus extra to decorate

5 eggs

3 tbsp melted coconut oil

1 tbsp honey

250g ground almonds

1 tsp ground cinnamon

1 tsp gluten-free baking powder

50g raisins

30g toasted flaked almonds

G P D

Preheat the oven to 180°C. Line a 1lb loaf tin with non-stick baking paper.

Spread the walnuts out on a baking tray and place in the oven for about 10 minutes, stirring them once or twice, until they are nicely toasted.

Whisk together the eggs, melted coconut oil and honey in a large bowl. Add the ground almonds, cinnamon and baking powder and mix into a thick batter. Stir in the toasted walnuts, the raisins and the flaked almonds.

Scrape the dough into the lined loaf tin and smooth the top with the back of a spoon. Decorate the top with a line of walnut halves down the middle. Bake in the oven for 35 minutes, until it's cooked through. Insert a knife or skewer into the centre to check it – if it comes out clean, it's ready. Turn it out of the baking tin and allow to cool on a wire rack.

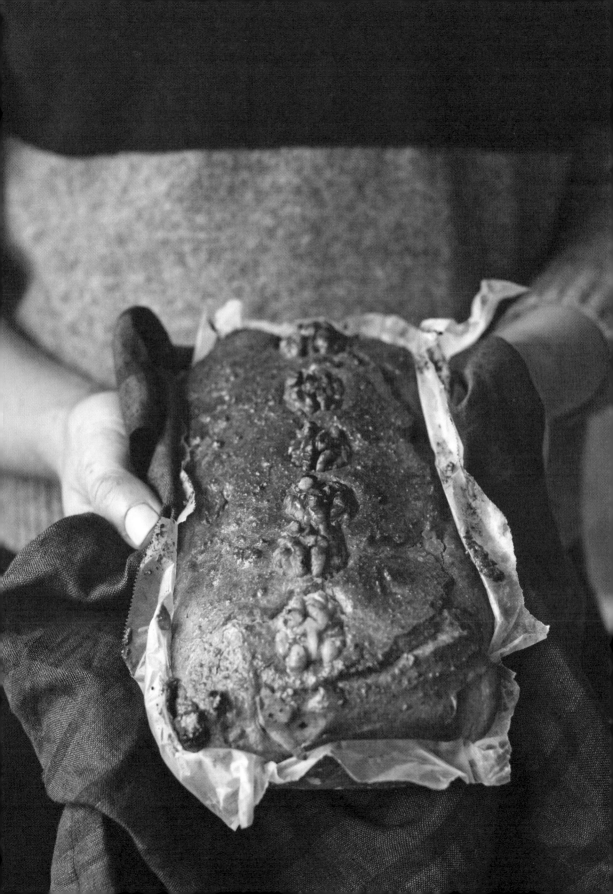

PEAR AND ALMOND SCONES

I love scones, but I thought a healthier version just wouldn't be the same.
How wrong I was! **MAKES 8 SCONES**

330g ground almonds, plus extra for dusting
....
2 tsp gluten-free baking powder
....
1 tsp ground cinnamon
....
2 eggs, lightly beaten
....
45g coconut oil (not melted)
....
1 ½ tbsp honey
....
½ small pear, peeled, cored and cut into cubes
....

Preheat the oven to 190°C. Line a baking tray with non-stick baking paper.

Mix together the ground almonds, baking powder and cinnamon in a large bowl. Add the beaten eggs, coconut oil and honey and use your hands to combine well to create a dough-like mixture. Add the chopped pear and use your hands again to mix it in. The dough should be wet enough that it sticks together easily.

Sprinkle some ground almonds on a wooden chopping board. Tip the dough out onto the board and pat it down until it's about 5cm thick. Use a fluted cutter or the rim of a glass to cut out the scones and place them on the lined baking tray.

Bake for 25 minutes, until set and lightly browned around the edges. Allow to cool on a wire rack. You can eat them straight away, while they're still warm from the oven, but I like to save them for breakfast the next morning and I reheat them in the microwave.

APPLE CINNAMON SCONES

Scones are a great way of making bread – they're instant portion control!

MAKES 8 SCONES

280g ground almonds, plus extra for dusting

120g coconut flour

2 tbsp gluten-free baking powder

1 tbsp ground cinnamon

3 eggs

3–4 tbsp honey (depending on how sweet you like it)

1½ tbsp melted butter or coconut oil

1 tsp almond essence

6 tbsp non-dairy milk (I use rice or almond milk)

1 apple, ½ grated and ½ cut into small chunks

handful of walnuts, broken into pieces

  P D

DAIRY FREE if you use coconut oil

Preheat the oven to 190°C. Line a baking tray with non-stick baking paper.

Stir together the ground almonds, coconut flour, baking powder and cinnamon in a large bowl.

In a separate bowl, whisk together the eggs, honey, melted butter or oil and the almond essence with a fork. Pour this into the bowl with the dry ingredients and mix everything together until it forms a slightly crumbly dough. Pour in the milk and mix again to form a dough. If it's too dry, add a little more milk to get a nice doughy consistency. If it's too wet, dust with a little more ground almonds until it's just right. Finally, use your hands to mix in the apple and walnuts and bring the dough together into a ball.

Sprinkle some ground almonds on a wooden chopping board. Tip the dough out onto the board and pat it down until it's about 5cm thick. Use a fluted cutter or the rim of a glass to cut out the scones and place them on the lined baking tray.

Bake for 15 minutes, then remove the tray from the oven and loosely cover it with a piece of tin foil so that the scones don't brown too much. Return the tray to the oven and bake for 10 minutes more, until the scones are cooked through. Let the scones cool on a wire rack, but if I were you I'd have one straight from the oven and leave the rest to cool.

LEMON, BLUEBERRY AND BANANA MUFFINS

Everyone should have one easy muffin mix in their repertoire. These are jam packed with all my favourite ingredients and the topping gives them an awesome sweet crust.

MAKES 16 MUFFINS

250g ground almonds

75g coconut flour

1 ½ tsp gluten-free baking powder

1 tsp gluten-free baking soda

1 tsp ground cinnamon

4 eggs

3 small or medium bananas, peeled

130g honey

60ml unsweetened almond milk

zest and juice of 1 lemon

3 tbsp coconut oil, melted

½ tsp vanilla essence

250g fresh blueberries

125g pecans, roughly chopped into quarters

30g banana chips, broken into pieces, to decorate

coconut sugar, to decorate

Preheat the oven to 180°C. Grease a muffin tin with a little coconut oil or use bun cases.

Combine the ground almonds, coconut flour, baking powder, baking soda and cinnamon in a large mixing bowl.

Put the eggs, bananas, honey, almond milk, lemon juice, melted coconut oil and vanilla in a blender and blitz until it's a smooth batter. Pour this into the dry ingredients and use a fork to give it a good stir until it's a smooth, thick batter. Switch to a spoon to stir in the blueberries, 100g of the pecans and the lemon zest.

Spoon approximately 2 heaped tablespoons of the batter into each case. Top each one with the remaining pecans, banana chips and a sprinkle of coconut sugar.

Bake in the oven for 25 minutes, then loosely cover with tin foil and bake for 10 minutes more – they will be toasted and crisp on top. Let the muffins cool on a wire rack for at least 15 minutes. Store in an airtight container at room temperature for up to five days.

SPORTS SNACKS

Fuelling your body for sports is something I had to learn a lot about during my triathlon training. I had a bit of an issue with shop-bought energy bars and gels, so I began creating my own. If I'm going to fuel my body for peak performance, I want it to be with foods I know and trust, not E numbers and additives.

WHATEVER YOU'RE INTO GRANOLA BARS

My favourite combination for these granola bars is cacao nibs, finely chopped dates and pecans. The cacao nibs are bitter, but they have a great crunch and taste like dark chocolate. But you can add whatever you like or whatever is in your kitchen press. Get creative in the kitchen and use this as a template to create your favourite breakfast bar on the go. The possibilities are endless! **MAKES 8 BARS**

2 tbsp coconut oil

1–2 tbsp honey or maple syrup (depending on how sweet you like it)

190g gluten-free oats

70g flaxseeds (I prefer whole flaxseeds, but milled flaxseeds are fine too)

1 tsp almond or vanilla essence (I prefer almond)

pinch of sea salt

125ml coconut water

OPTIONAL EXTRAS:

chopped nuts

chopped dried fruit

handful of cacao nibs

coconut chips

goji berries

chia seeds

VEGAN if you use maple syrup

Preheat the oven to 190°C. Line a 2lb loaf tin with non-stick baking paper.

Put the coconut oil and honey in a large bowl and zap it in the microwave for 40–60 seconds, until melted. Stir in the oats, flaxseeds, almond essence and a pinch of sea salt. Add all your chosen extras and just enough coconut water for it all to stick together a little (125ml coconut water is usually enough). The coconut water gives a lovely moistness to the finished bar and adds some natural sweetness and potassium too.

Scrape into the lined tin and bake for 35–40 minutes, until golden brown on top and hard when tapped. If you think the dried fruit or nuts are getting a little burnt (don't worry, this can happen!), loosely cover the tin with foil. Leave to cool in the tin for 1 hour before cutting into bars, if you can resist them that long!

SUPER CRUNCH GRANOLA BARS

The crunch in these bars is so satisfying that it's hard to stop at just one. They're great for snacking on or broken up as granola bites in a bowl of almond milk. Use whatever combination of seeds and nuts you like. I use sunflower seeds, pumpkin seeds, sesame seeds, macadamia nuts, hazelnuts and pistachios and I chop the larger nuts. Or you can make these nut-free by replacing the nuts with more seeds. **MAKES 12 BARS**

2 tbsp coconut oil, plus extra for greasing

130g light tahini

150ml honey or maple syrup

200g nut and seed mix (see note above)

100g mix of rice flakes and millet flakes

70g raw mulberries (or your favourite dried fruit)

50g buckwheat groats

35g cacao nibs

handful of coconut chips

1 tbsp ground cinnamon

Preheat the oven to 180°C. Grease a 20cm square baking tin with a little coconut oil.

Melt the coconut oil in a large saucepan set over a medium heat. Add the tahini and sweetener and bring up to a gentle simmer, stirring constantly so that it doesn't stick to the bottom of the pan. It should resemble a thick sauce. Remove the pan from the heat, add the remaining dry ingredients and combine until everything is evenly mixed.

Scrape into the greased baking tin. Using the back of a spatula, press down firmly until the bars are 2.5cm thick. It's really important that you press them down to ensure they are compact and won't fall apart.

Bake for 20 minutes, until evenly toasted. Let them cool fully in the tin before cutting into bars to make sure it sets.

VEGAN if you use maple syrup

CRUNCH TIME

Beat the bonk with these homemade energy bars! This is my favourite no-bake bar, both on and off the bike. It's a complete gear changer. **MAKES 12 BARS**

100g dark chocolate (at least 70% cocoa solids), broken into pieces

200g smooth or crunchy peanut butter

200g honey

2 scoops (60g) vanilla whey protein powder

180g gluten-free oats

70g puffed cereal (such as brown rice)

50g buckwheat groats

Line a 20cm x 20cm square baking tin with non-stick baking paper.

Melt the chocolate in a heatproof bowl set over a pan of gently simmering water (a bain-marie), making sure the water doesn't touch the bottom of the bowl. Stir until smooth.

Mix together the peanut butter, honey and whey protein powder in a large bowl until smooth. It should resemble a thick batter. Add the oats and mix well again, then stir in three-quarters of the melted chocolate. Gently mix in the puffed cereal and the buckwheat groats using your hands.

Spoon the mixture into the lined baking tin and press it down firmly to create a level surface. Drizzle the remaining dark chocolate all over the top. Put the tin in the fridge for 30–40 minutes, until the bars have set. Cut into 12 bars and store in an airtight container in the fridge for up to two weeks.

OAT AND FRUIT BARS

Medjool dates are a great sweetener for sports bars because they replenish energy levels instantly and are a good source of potassium too, which helps to regulate heart rate and blood pressure. **MAKES 6 LARGE BARS**

180g gluten-free oats

200g Medjool dates, pitted

250ml coconut water

pinch of sea salt

1 tsp ground nutmeg (optional)

1 tsp ground cinnamon (optional)

1 tsp mixed spice (optional)

110g raw pecans, broken into pieces

80g raisins (optional)

Preheat the oven to 200°C. Line a 20cm x 20cm square baking tin with non-stick baking paper.

Place the oats in a food processor and blend until a fine flour forms, then tip into a bowl. Add the dates and coconut water to the food processor and blend until it turns into a smooth caramel. Add a pinch of sea salt and the spices, if using, and blend again just to combine.

Mix the date caramel with the oat flour until it's fully combined (it should look like a heavy paste), then stir in the pecans and the raisins, if using. Spoon into the lined baking tin and press down using the back of the spoon to create a level top.

Bake for 17–20 minutes, keeping an eye on them towards the end of the cooking time. If you think the top is getting too browned, loosely cover the tin with foil. They should look nice and crisp on top and still be a little moist on the inside. Cool on a wire rack for 15 minutes before cutting into bars. Store in an airtight container in the fridge for up to six days.

MUSCLE MUNCH

You could literally stick one of these bars in your back pocket all day and it won't melt or go soggy. The other great thing about them is that you can either eat them raw or baked – it's up to you! **MAKES 10 BARS**

200g gluten-free rolled oats

250g Medjool dates, pitted

2 scoops (50g) brown rice protein powder (I use That Protein brand)

1 banana, peeled

125ml unsweetened almond milk

150g chopped toasted nuts

Line a 20cm x 20cm square baking tin with non-stick baking paper.

Place the oats in a food processor and blend until a fine flour forms, then add the pitted dates and blend again until it forms a smooth dough. Add the brown rice powder, banana and almond milk and blend into a wet dough with no lumps or traces of dates or banana. Stir in the chopped nuts.

Spoon into the lined baking tin and press down using the back of the spoon to create a level top. You can either let these sit in the fridge for about 1 hour, until they've firmed up, and eat them raw, or you can pop the bars into an oven preheated to 180°C for 8 minutes, until they're firm on the outside and an outer crust has formed. Let them cool fully in the tin before cutting into bars. Store in an airtight container in the fridge for up to four days.

BUCKWHEAT BOUNCE

These no-bake bars are a great time-saver for a busy triathlete, plus they last for over a week in the fridge. **MAKES 8 BARS**

150g buckwheat groats

75g raw almonds

55g raw pecans

250g Medjool dates, pitted

80g dried cranberries

4 tbsp hemp seeds

3 tbsp milled flaxseeds

1 ½ tbsp raw cacao powder

Preheat the oven to 190°C. Line a 2lb loaf tin with non-stick baking paper.

Put 50g of the buckwheat groats on one baking tray and the almonds and pecans on a separate tray. Toast them all in the oven for about 10 minutes.

Put all the ingredients except the toasted buckwheat into a food processor and blend until it's almost smooth – you want to leave a little bit of crunch. This should take 2–5 minutes, depending on how powerful your food processor is. Now stir in the toasted buckwheat.

Press the mixture firmly into the lined loaf tin and refrigerate for at least 3 hours, until set, or place in the freezer for 20–25 minutes. Store them in an airtight container in the fridge for up to 10 days.

SWEET AND SALTY NUT-FREE TRAIL MIX

I like to use my own blend of seeds for this trail mix, but you can substitute 50g of a good ready-made seed mix instead. I really do bring this everywhere with me, and anyone who sneaks a handful of it when I'm on a photo shoot gets hooked too. **MAKES 140G**

15g pumpkin seeds

15g sunflower seeds

2 tbsp flaxseeds

1 tbsp linseeds

1 tbsp tamari, gluten-free soya sauce or Braggs Liquid Aminos

3 dates, pitted and chopped

2 dried apricots, chopped (optional)

20g coconut chips (unsulphured if possible)

1 tbsp goji berries

1 tbsp cacao nibs

pinch of sea salt

Preheat the oven to 190°C.

Spread out all the seeds on a baking tray and toast them in the oven for 5 minutes. Remove the tray from the oven and drizzle over the tamari. Mix it around to make sure all the seeds are coated, then return the tray to the oven and toast the seeds for 2–3 minutes more. Set aside to let them cool.

Put the cooled toasted seeds in a bowl and mix in the remaining ingredients until everything is well combined into a sweet and salty mix. Transfer the trail mix to an airtight container and use within two weeks.

TROPICAL TRAIL MIX

The perfect snack to get you in the holiday mood! This is my number one airport essential. It keeps for weeks, so make extra for the journey home. **MAKES 85G**

50g mix of dried mango and pineapple

20g raw macadamia nuts

15g toasted coconut chips

Simply mix all the ingredients together and store in an airtight container for up to one month.

284

295

290

DIPS
AND THINGS

Making your own sauces, spreads and dips can make a big change to your diet. By adding a little extra oomph to any snack or meal, they are a vital component to healthy eating.

QUICK HUMMUS

Hummus is so easy to whip up and it's a handy dip to have in the fridge when you're feeling peckish. Try it with some raw vegetable sticks or the herbed cracker thins on page 192. It works well with roasted veg too. **MAKES 250G**

1 x 400g tin of chickpeas, drained and rinsed

1 garlic clove, peeled

juice of ½ lemon

2 tbsp olive oil

1 tsp ground cumin

sea salt and freshly ground black pepper

Put all the ingredients in a food processor and blend until smooth. Stored in an airtight container in the fridge, this hummus will keep for up to six days.

ROASTED CARROT HUMMUS

I test all my hummus recipes on my sister – you could say she's a bit of a hummus addict – and this one is her favourite. **MAKES 250G**

1 medium carrot, cut into cubes

1 tsp ground coriander

½ tsp ground cinnamon

sea salt and freshly ground black pepper

1 x 400g tin of chickpeas, drained and rinsed

1 garlic clove, peeled

juice of ½ lemon

2 tbsp olive oil

Preheat the oven to 190°C. Put the carrot cubes on a baking tray, sprinkle with the coriander and cumin and season with salt and pepper (you don't need to use any oil). Roast for 35–40 minutes, until soft and golden. Let them cool, then put in a food processor with the remaining ingredients and blend until smooth. Stored in an airtight container in the fridge, this hummus will keep for up to six days.

MISO HUMMUS

MAKES 250G

1 x 400g tin of chickpeas, drained and rinsed

....

1 garlic clove, peeled

....

juice of ½ lemon

....

2 tbsp olive oil

....

1 tbsp freshly squeezed orange juice

....

1 tsp tamari

....

1 tsp miso paste

....

sea salt and freshly ground black pepper

....

Put all the ingredients in a food processor and blend until smooth. Stored in an airtight container in the fridge, this hummus will keep for up to six days.

AVOCADO AND FETA DIP

This is *the* best dip. I once made it during a supermarket demo and I still get emails looking for the recipe, so here you go! **MAKES 150G**

1 ripe avocado, peeled and stoned
....
50g feta cheese
....
20g fresh dill
....
1 garlic clove, peeled
....
juice of ½ lemon
....
30g raw cashews
....
pinch of sea salt
....

Put the avocado, feta, dill, garlic and lemon juice in a food processor and blend until smooth. Add the cashews and blend again for 10–15 seconds just to break up the nuts. This is best served straight away, otherwise the avocado in the dip will start to turn brown.

GUACAMOLE

I know there are thousands of guac recipes out there already, but can you ever really have enough? **MAKES 250G**

2 ripe avocados, peeled, stoned and mashed
....
1 red onion, finely diced
....
1 ripe tomato, diced
....
1 garlic clove, crushed
....
juice of 1 lime
....
3 tbsp finely chopped fresh coriander
....
sea salt and freshly ground black pepper
....

Mash all the ingredients together in a pestle and mortar. If you want to make this a little bit ahead of time, keep the avocado stones in the guacamole bowl and cover it with cling film to keep it fresh for longer, otherwise it can turn brown.

BUTTERBEAN AND SUN-DRIED TOMATO DIP

Serve with vegetable batons or the herbed cracker thins on page 192. Believe it or not, it's also really good alongside a steak. **MAKES 250G**

1 x 400g tin of butterbeans, drained and rinsed
....
5 sun-dried tomatoes preserved in olive oil
....
1 garlic clove, peeled
....
2 tbsp freshly squeezed lemon juice
....
1 tbsp extra virgin olive oil
....
1 tsp chilli flakes
....
20g fresh coriander
....
sea salt and freshly ground black pepper
....

Put everything into a food processor and blend until the dip is smooth and thick. Store in an airtight container or jar in the fridge for up to three days.

 G V D

MINTY PEA DIP

Awesome with any fish or meat dishes. **MAKES 450G**

400g frozen peas

1 garlic clove, peeled

juice of 1 lemon

1 tbsp Greek yoghurt or light tahini (optional)

1 tbsp chopped fresh flat-leaf parsley

3 fresh mint leaves

Pour the peas into a bowl and cover them with hot water. Once they have completely thawed, drain them well and pat dry with a clean tea towel. Put the thawed peas in a food processor with the rest of the ingredients. Blend for about 40 seconds, until the dip is smooth and thick. Store in an airtight container or jar in the fridge for up to three days.

DAIRY FREE if you use tahini

VEGAN if you use tahini

BLACK BEAN DIP

My obsession with black bean dip began when I was modelling in New York. It might come as no surprise that the only real memories I have of my time there are all of the wonderful food I discovered! This dip works really well with shredded chicken.

MAKES 200G

1 x 400g tin of black beans, drained and rinsed

25g fresh coriander leaves

1 jalapeño, deseeded

1 garlic clove, peeled

juice of ½ lime

1 tsp chilli powder

Put everything in a food processor and blend until the dip is smooth and thick. Store in an airtight container or jar in the fridge for up to three days.

BLACK BEAN, MANGO AND AVOCADO SALSA

This colourful, flavourful salsa is great little extra alongside chilli. **SERVES 4**

1 x 400g tin of black beans, drained and rinsed

1 mango, peeled and diced

1 ripe avocado, peeled, stoned and cubed

½ red onion, finely chopped

25g fresh coriander, chopped

juice of 1 lime

sea salt and freshly ground black pepper

(G)(V)(D)

To make the salsa, just combine all the ingredients in a mixing bowl and season to taste. Let it sit at room temperature for at least 30 minutes to allow the flavours to develop.

CASHEW CHEESE WITH SWEET RED PEPPER

One of the most versatile nuts around, cashews are incredibly easy to eat too much of! I suggest serving this cashew cheese in small ramekins to help with portion control. But maybe that's just me. **MAKES 350ML**

250g raw cashews

1 large sweet red pepper, halved and deseeded

1 tbsp extra virgin olive oil

sea salt and freshly ground black pepper

250ml filtered water

3 tbsp nutritional yeast

2 tbsp freshly squeezed lemon juice

Put the cashews in a small bowl, cover them with water and let them soak for at least 2 hours.

Preheat the oven to 200°C. Place the halved sweet red pepper on a baking tray, drizzle with the oil, season well and cook for 25 minutes, until softened and lightly browned.

Drain the cashews and put them in a food processor along with the roasted pepper and its juices and the filtered water. Blend together until there are no bits – it should be like a thick cream. Add the nutritional yeast and lemon juice and blend again. The final dip should resemble a thick, creamy sauce. Add a little more water if it looks too dry. Serve alongside the herbed cracker thins on page 192 or vegetable batons. Store in a large jar in the fridge for up to three days.

SAVOURY CASHEW CHEESE

Nutritional yeast has a cheesy flavour, which makes it a great dairy-free, vegan addition to sauces and soups. It's inactive, so it's still suitable for people who avoid yeast.

MAKES 350ML

250g raw cashews

1 garlic glove, peeled

250ml vegetable stock

juice of ½ lemon

2 tbsp nutritional yeast

1 tsp Dijon mustard

Put the cashews in a small bowl, cover them with water and let them soak for at least 2 hours. Drain the cashews and put them in a food processor or blender along with the remaining ingredients. Blitz until it becomes a soft spread. This is perfect served with grilled vegetables, crackers or rice cakes. Store in a large jar in the fridge for up to three days.

RED ONION MARMALADE

Red onion marmalade goes with everything and helps to liven up plain meals. It's especially delicious served with steak and the herbed cracker thins on page 192.

MAKES SMALL 1 JAR

1 tbsp coconut oil
....

2 red onions, finely chopped
....

2 tbsp honey, maple syrup
or coconut nectar
....

1 tsp ground cinnamon
....

1 tsp balsamic cider vinegar
or regular balsamic vinegar
....

VEGAN if you use maple
syrup or coconut nectar

Melt the coconut oil in a saucepan over a low heat. Sweat the onions for 10 minutes, until they are softened but not browned. Add the honey, cinnamon and vinegar and cook for 5 minutes more, until it has thickened. Remove from the heat and transfer to a food processor and blend briefly, until broken down but not smooth – you want to keep a bit of texture. Spoon into a clean jar and store in the fridge for up to one week.

APRICOT CHUTNEY

Growing up in the country, I couldn't open a press without at least three jars of chutney falling out of it, so it's always been something that I've added to my plate. My recipe avoids all the additional sugars in some store-bought chutneys. **MAKES 1 SMALL JAR**

6 dried apricots

½ red onion, finely chopped

½ jalapeño, deseeded and finely chopped

juice of ½ lemon

3 tbsp honey or maple syrup

2 tbsp apple cider vinegar

2 tbsp raisins (optional)

  G V P D

VEGAN if you use maple syrup

Put all the ingredients in a small saucepan. Bring to a boil, then reduce the heat to a simmer and cook for 20 minutes, until everything is soft. Blitz with a hand-held blender for just 5–10 seconds, so it's still chunky. Spoon into a clean jar and store in the fridge for up to three days.

FIERY RELISH

I love relish, but I hate looking at the labels on shop-bought ones. This raw relish is so easy to whip up and it's a handy thing to have a jar of in your fridge. **MAKES 1 MEDIUM JAR**

75g sun-dried tomatoes preserved in olive oil
....

6 cherry tomatoes, halved
....

1 red pepper, deseeded and finely chopped
....

1 large fresh red chilli, deseeded and finely chopped
....

2 Medjool dates, pitted
....

2 tbsp raisins (optional)
....

1 tbsp mustard seeds
....

2 tsp apple cider vinegar
....

1 tsp ground cinnamon
....

1 tsp ground cumin
....

1 tsp sweet paprika
....

Place all the ingredients in a food processor and blend for a minute into a smooth, thick spread. Store in an airtight container or jar in the fridge for up to one week.

 G V P D

HOMEMADE MAYO

Homemade mayonnaise is quick and easy to make and is so much better than anything shop bought. **MAKES 450G (2 MEDIUM JARS)**

2 egg yolks

2 tbsp apple cider vinegar

1 tsp Dijon mustard

5–7 tbsp olive oil or nut oil

1 tbsp chopped fresh dill or chives (optional if using for the savoury oatcakes with smoked salmon on page 062)

Put the egg yolks, vinegar and mustard in a large bowl and whisk them together until well combined (an electric whisk works well for this). Slowly add the oil a little at a time while whisking continuously. It should start to get thick. Keep adding the oil, bit by bit, until you reach your desired consistency. Spoon into a clean glass jar and store in the fridge for up to five days.

GARLIC 'MAYO'

Probiotic yoghurt can be a great source of good gut bacteria. Look for a high-quality yoghurt with live cultures – the fewer ingredients, the better. I'm all about good gut health! **MAKES 200G (1 MEDIUM JAR)**

125ml unsweetened probiotic yoghurt

1 large garlic glove, crushed

juice of ½ lemon

½ tsp mixed dried herbs

¼ tsp onion powder

¼ tsp garlic powder

pinch of sea salt

Place all the ingredients in a mixing bowl and whisk them together with a fork. Spoon into a clean glass jar and keep in the fridge for up to three days.

VEGAN PESTO

This crunchy vegan pesto is a breeze to whip up and it works brilliantly with spiralised vegetable noodles – try it with the rainbow 'spaghetti' on page 166. **MAKES 165G**

45g shelled pistachios

80g fresh basil leaves

2 garlic cloves, peeled

4 tbsp extra virgin olive oil or avocado oil

3 tbsp nutritional yeast

1 tbsp freshly squeezed lemon juice

To toast the pistachios, heat a heavy-based, dry frying pan over a medium heat. Add the nuts and cook, stirring, for a few minutes, just until they start to brown.

Put the nuts into a food processor along with all the other ingredients and blend for 40–60 seconds (or longer if you want a smoother pesto). Spoon into a clean glass jar and cover the top with a thin film of oil so that it doesn't turn brown. Store in the fridge for up to one week.

THE BEST STIR-FRY DRESSING

Sometimes all you need are one or two dressing recipes that can tart up any type of meal – like this one! **MAKES 170ML**

½ stalk of fresh lemongrass

2.5cm piece of fresh root ginger, peeled and minced

juice of 2 limes

3 tbsp tamari

2 tbsp maple syrup

1 tbsp sesame oil

1 tbsp apple cider vinegar

Remove the outer leaves from the lemongrass stalk and cut away the tough upper half and the base. Cut the stalk in half to reveal the tender core and finely dice this white part. Put the lemongrass into a clean screw-top jar along with the rest of the ingredients. Screw on the lid and shake to combine. Store in the fridge for up to five days, giving it a good shake again before using.

QUICK AND EASY PASSATA

If you make only one thing from scratch, make this simple passata. You can use it as a pasta sauce, pizza sauce or with spiralised vegetable noodles. It's easy to scale up if you want to make larger batches and it freezes brilliantly too. **MAKES 600ML**

8 ripe plum tomatoes, halved
....
6 ripe cherry tomatoes
....
sea salt and freshly ground black pepper
....

Preheat the oven to 190°C. Put the tomatoes on a baking tray and roast for 20 minutes, until the skins have split and the tomatoes are soft. Scrape the tomatoes into a blender along with their juices and blitz until smooth, then season to taste. Store in a glass jar in the fridge for up to four days.

RED PEPPER PASSATA

The red peppers give a creamy, sweet finish to this passata. **MAKES 450ML**

4 ripe plum tomatoes, halved
....
2 red peppers, deseeded and halved
....
1 tsp rapeseed oil
....
sea salt and freshly ground black pepper
....

Preheat the oven to 190°C. Put the tomatoes and peppers on a baking tray, drizzle with the oil and roast for 25 minutes, until browned on top and the peppers have wilted. Scrape into a blender along with all the juices and blitz until smooth, then season to taste. Store in a glass jar in the fridge for up to four days.

SIMPLE RED PEPPER SAUCE

My favourite sauce to serve with courgetti. **MAKES 250ML**

1 sweet red pepper,
deseeded and halved
....

1 red bell pepper, deseeded
and halved
....

1 tbsp rapeseed oil or
melted coconut oil
....

sea salt and freshly ground
black pepper
....

Preheat the oven to 190°C. Put the halved peppers on a baking tray, drizzle with the oil and season well with salt and pepper. Roast for 20 minutes, until softened and browned. Scrape into a food processor along with all the cooking juices and blend until smooth. I like my sauce thick, but if you want it thin, add 50ml of warm water and blend again. Store in a glass jar in the fridge for up to four days.

RASPBERRY JAM

I love a spoonful of this jam over my porridge or served with peanut butter on sliced bananas. Agar agar is a Japanese plant-based gelling agent available in all health food stores and good supermarkets. It's what gives this jam its fabulous jelly-like texture.

MAKES 1 LARGE OR 2 SMALL JARS

350g fresh raspberries

125ml freshly squeezed orange juice

3 tbsp honey or maple syrup

2 tbsp chia seeds

1 tsp vanilla essence

3 tbsp agar agar flakes

VEGAN if you use maple syrup

Put the raspberries and orange juice in a saucepan over a very low heat and simmer for 8–10 minutes, stirring constantly, until the raspberries have broken down into a liquid. If you want a smoother jam, you can strain it through a fine-mesh sieve at this point to get rid of the raspberry seeds and then return it to the pan. Stir in the honey, chia seeds and vanilla, then add the agar agar flakes. Turn up the heat and bring to a boil. Keep stirring for 3–5 minutes more, until the agar agar flakes have dissolved. Spoon into a clean jar, screw on the lid and pop in the fridge overnight to let the jam set. This jam will keep in the fridge for up to one week.

QUICK BLUEBERRY CHIA JAM

Did you know that 'chia' is the ancient Mayan word for strength? Packed full of fibre, omega-3s and protein, these seeds are amongst the most nutritious foods on the planet. Small but mighty! **MAKES 1 SMALL JAR**

150g fresh blueberries
(raspberries work well too)
....
1 tbsp chia seeds
....
1 tbsp freshly squeezed
lemon juice
....
½ tsp honey or maple syrup
....

VEGAN if you use maple syrup

Put the berries in a bowl and microwave them for 40–60 seconds or place them in a small saucepan and simmer over a medium-low heat for about 5 minutes, until the berries have started to break down and release their juices. Mash them with a fork, then stir in the chia seeds, lemon juice and honey. Spoon into a clean jar and pop in the fridge for at least 30 minutes before using to give the chia seeds enough time to swell up and give it a nice jam-like consistency. Stored in the fridge, this jam will last for up to three days.

ORANGE SAFFRON MARMALADE

Homemade jam or marmalade may seem like a lot of fuss to make yourself, but you'll have this made in less time than it takes to go to the shop to buy some. **MAKES 1 LARGE JAR**

4 large oranges, washed, peeled and sliced (save the rinds)
....
500ml water
....
80g honey or maple syrup
....
pinch of saffron
....
2 tbsp agar agar flakes
....

....
VEGAN if you use maple syrup

Place the sliced oranges and the water in a saucepan along with the rinds from two of the oranges. Cut the rind of one of the remaining oranges into thick or thin slices, depending on how you like your marmalade, and set these aside. Bring to the boil, then reduce the heat and simmer for 10–15 minutes, stirring, until the oranges have broken down and almost dissolved. Strain through a piece of cheesecloth, muslin cloth or a jelly bag. Place the sieved orange juice back into the pan and add the honey and saffron. Bring up to a simmer again, then stir in the agar agar and let it cook for about 2 minutes, until the agar agar has dissolved. Stir in the sliced orange rinds that you set aside earlier.

Spoon the marmalade into a clean glass jar and screw on the lid. Allow it to cool before putting it in the fridge to set. Stored in the fridge, this marmalade will keep for up to 10 days.

CASHEW CREAM

Make this once, and you'll be hooked. You can't say I didn't warn you! It's the perfect topping for pancakes, fresh fruit or granola – or for eating straight from the jar with a spoon. **MAKES 600G**

250g raw cashews

250ml filtered water

juice of ½ lemon

1 vanilla pod, split in half lengthways, seeds scraped out and pod discarded

1 ½ tbsp honey or maple syrup

Put the cashews in a small bowl, cover them with water and let them soak for at least 4–5 hours. Drain the cashews and put them in a food processor or blender along with all the other ingredients and blitz until smooth. Spoon into a clean jar and store in the fridge for up to four days.

VEGAN if you use maple syrup

COCO CREAM

I used to love whipped cream, so creating this tropical substitute was one of my best kitchen experiments. **MAKES 300ML**

1 x 400ml tin of full-fat coconut milk

zest of 1 lime

1 tbsp maple syrup

1 vanilla pod, split in half lengthways, seeds scraped out and pod discarded

Pop the tin of coconut milk in the freezer for at least 20 minutes so that the cream separates from the rest of the milk. Open the tin just a little and strain out the liquid, leaving only the thick cream. (You can use this thin milk for smoothies.) Scoop the cream out of the tin and put it in a bowl. It should be the consistency of thick cream.

Using a hand-held electric whisk, slowly add the lime zest, maple syrup and vanilla seeds, whisking continuously until the coconut cream thickens and forms soft peaks. Spoon into a clean jar and store in the fridge for up to three days.

THE NUT BUTTER COLLECTIVE

Nut butters are the best companion for any sort of snack, for making bars, for adding a little something extra to dishes or just simply eating straight out of the jar with a spoon.

Note: You need a powerful, high-speed blender (like a Thermomix or Vitamix) for making most of these nut butters, otherwise you risk breaking your blender, trust me! Peanuts are a little softer and easier to break down than other nuts, so you don't need to spend hundreds of euros on a high-power food processor to make your own peanut butter – your regular blender or food processor will do the trick.

CARAMEL PEANUT SPREAD

I used to hate peanut butter and couldn't understand how anyone could like it. But after moving to New York and eventually being convinced to give it a go, I became addicted and now I'm a total 'peanutter'. **MAKES 2 LARGE JARS**

500g skinned, unsalted peanuts
....
4 Medjool dates, pitted
....
pinch of sea salt (optional)
....

Preheat the oven to 200°C.

Spread the peanuts out on a baking tray and toast them in the oven for about 10 minutes, stirring them halfway through.

Place the toasted nuts in a food processor (or a high-speed blender works well too if you have one) and blitz for 6–8 minutes, stopping to scrape down the sides if necessary. Once you have a smooth, creamy texture, add the Medjool dates and a pinch of sea salt, if using, and blend again until the dates are completely broken down – you don't want any bits or lumps. I have to blend this for a good 12–15 minutes in total, so keep at it! Spoon into a clean jar and store at room temperature for up to two weeks.

CHOCOLATE PEANUT SPREAD

MAKES 2 SMALL JARS

350g skinned, unsalted
peanuts
....
1 ½ tbsp raw cacao powder
....
1 tbsp honey or maple syrup
....

....
VEGAN if you use maple syrup

Preheat the oven to 200°C.

Spread the peanuts out on a baking tray and toast them in the oven for about 10 minutes, stirring them halfway through.

Place the toasted nuts in a food processor (or a high-speed blender works well too if you have one) and blitz for 6–8 minutes, stopping to scrape down the sides if necessary. Once you have a smooth, creamy texture, add the cacao powder and sweetener. Continue blending until it's a nice, creamy spread – this could take up to 15 minutes in total, so keep at it – scraping down the sides again if necessary. Spoon into a clean jar and store at room temperature for up to two weeks.

PEANUT BUTTER WITH MAPLE SYRUP AND CINNAMON

Unlike other nut butters, it's hard to find brands of peanut butter that are whole and natural, so I recommend making your own. **MAKES 2 LARGE JARS**

500g skinned, unsalted peanuts

3 tbsp maple syrup

2 tbsp ground cinnamon

Preheat the oven to 200°C.

Put the peanuts in a bowl and pour the maple syrup over them. Sprinkle in the cinnamon and mix well until the peanuts are evenly coated. Spread the peanuts out on a baking tray and toast them in the oven for about 10 minutes, stirring them halfway through.

Place the toasted nuts in a food processor (or a high-speed blender works well too if you have one) and blend on full power for 12–15 minutes, stopping to scrape down the sides if necessary, until it's smooth and creamy. Spoon into a clean jar and store at room temperature for up to two weeks.

SPICY PEANUT BUTTER

The great thing about nuts is the fact that they're so versatile. Take this nut butter – they are usually sweet, but this savoury option is delicious with eggs, salmon or on crackers.

MAKES 2 LARGE JARS

500g skinned, roasted, unsalted peanuts
....
1 tsp cayenne pepper
....
½ tsp chilli powder
....
½ tsp smoked paprika
....
pinch of sea salt
....

Blend all the ingredients in a food processor (or a high-speed blender works well too if you have one) on full power for 12–15 minutes, stopping to scrape down the sides if necessary, until it's smooth and creamy. Spoon into a clean jar and store at room temperature for up to two weeks.

CHOCOLATE ALMOND BUTTER

MAKES 2 LARGE JARS

300g raw almonds

200g raw hazelnuts

1 ½ tbsp raw cacao powder

1 tbsp honey, maple syrup or coconut nectar

VEGAN if you use maple syrup or coconut nectar

Preheat the oven to 200°C.

Put the almonds on one baking tray and the hazelnuts on a separate tray. Place them in the oven and toast them for about 10 minutes, stirring them halfway through. The hazelnuts may need a few minutes more, until the skins have started to loosen. Remove the hazelnut skins using the roast-and-rub method: tip the warm nuts into a slightly dampened clean kitchen towel, fold up the sides and rub the skins off using the towel.

Place the toasted nuts in a powerful, high-speed blender and blend for 8–10 minutes, stopping to scrape down the sides if necessary, until it's smooth and almost liquid. Add the cacao powder and sweetener and blend again for another 6–8 minutes. The nut butter will get thick again, but keep blending until it goes back to that nice liquid consistency. Spoon into a clean jar and store in the fridge for up to two weeks.

CARAMEL PECAN SPREAD

MAKES 2 LARGE JARS

300g raw pecans

200g raw almonds

2 Medjool dates, pitted

pinch of sea salt

pinch of ground cinnamon (optional)

Preheat the oven to 200°C.

Spread the nuts out on a baking tray and toast them in the oven for about 10 minutes, stirring them halfway through.

Place all the ingredients into a powerful, high-speed blender and blend continuously for 8–12 minutes, stopping to scrape down the sides if necessary, until a smooth, creamy spread forms. Spoon into a clean jar and store in the fridge for up to one week.

NOTELLA

MAKES 2 LARGE JARS

60g cacao butter

500g skinned, toasted hazelnuts

2 tbsp maple syrup

1 tbsp raw cacao powder

1 vanilla pod, split in half lengthways, seeds scraped out and pod discarded

Put the cacao butter in a heatproof bowl and zap it in the microwave for 1–2 minutes, until melted.

Put the hazelnuts into a high-speed blender and blitz until the nuts break down and start to form a smooth spread. Add the melted cacao butter, maple syrup, cacao powder and vanilla seeds and blend again. It will dry out initially, but keep blending for 8–10 minutes, until it turns creamy again.

Spoon into a clean jar and store in the fridge for up to two weeks. It will harden up, so leave it at room temperature for 20 minutes before serving it if you want a softer spread.

CHOCOLATE PECAN SPREAD

MAKES 2 LARGE JARS

350g raw pecans

200g raw almonds

1 tbsp maple syrup

1 tsp raw cacao powder

Preheat the oven to 200°C.

Spread the nuts out on a baking tray and toast them in the oven for about 10 minutes, stirring them halfway through.

Place the toasted nuts in a powerful, high-speed blender and blend for 8–10 minutes, stopping to scrape down the sides if necessary, until it's smooth and almost liquid. Add the maple syrup and cacao powder and blend again for another 6–8 minutes. The nut butter will get thick again, but keep blending until it goes back to that nice liquid consistency. Spoon into a clean jar and store at room temperature for up to one week, or it will last a little longer if you keep it in the fridge.

MACADAMIA NUT BUTTER

MAKES 2 MEDIUM JARS

35g cacao butter

500g raw macadamia nuts

1 tbsp honey or maple syrup

VEGAN if you use maple syrup

Put the cacao butter in a heatproof bowl and zap it in the microwave for 1–2 minutes, until melted.

Put the macadamia nuts into a powerful, high-speed blender and blend for 10–12 minutes, stopping to scrape down the sides if necessary, until smooth and creamy. Pour in the melted cacao butter and stir in the sweetener and blend again for 1–2 minutes more, until everything is completely combined. Spoon into a clean jar and store at room temperature or in the fridge for a harder spread. Either way, it will last for up to two weeks.

ALL OR NUTTIN' BUTTER

MAKES 3 SMALL JARS

200g raw almonds

150g raw cashews

150g raw hazelnuts

70g mixed seeds (pumpkin, sunflower, flaxseed)

2 tbsp chia seeds

2 tbsp cacao nibs

pinch of sea salt

Preheat the oven to 180°C. Put the almonds and cashews on one baking tray and the hazelnuts on a separate tray. Toast them in the oven for about 10 minutes, stirring them halfway through. The hazelnuts may need a few minutes more, until the skins have started to loosen. Remove the hazelnut skins by tipping the warm nuts into a slightly dampened clean kitchen towel, then fold up the sides and rub the skins off using the towel. Set the nuts aside to let them cool.

Put the nuts and half of the mixed seeds into a powerful, high-speed blender and blitz for 6–8 minutes, stopping to scrape down the sides if necessary, until it starts to form a smooth butter. Scrape the butter into a mixing bowl.

Crush the remaining seeds in a pestle and mortar, then stir them into the nut butter with the chia seeds, cacao nibs and salt. Spoon into a clean jar and store in the fridge for up to two weeks.

SUPERSEED ME SPREAD

For the person in your life with a nut allergy, it's time they got to indulge in this spread. It's surprisingly awesome. Although it's green and extremely healthy looking, it's scarily easy to eat straight out of the jar, but it's also delicious with apple slices. **MAKES 1 LARGE JAR**

200g sunflower seeds
....

150g pumpkin seeds
....

1 tbsp honey or maple syrup
....

pinch of sea salt
....

VEGAN if you use maple syrup

Preheat the oven to 190°C.

Spread the seeds out over a baking tray and toast them in the oven for about 8 minutes, stirring them once or twice, until they are light golden all over.

While the seeds are still warm (the heat will help them break down), put them into a powerful, high-speed food processor with the honey and a pinch of sea salt and blend until smooth and dreamy. Don't try to use a blender to make this spread – the seeds are too hard for a blender to break down. Spoon into a clean jar and store in the fridge for up to two weeks.

INDEX